# Musings from a Healing Heart

# Musings from a Healing Heart

*Betty Bennett*

iUniverse, Inc.

New York Lincoln Shanghai

# Musings from a Healing Heart

iUniverse, Inc.

For information address:
iUniverse, Inc.
2021 Pine Lake Road, Suite 100
Lincoln, NE 68512
www.iuniverse.com

ISBN: 0-595-27402-1

Printed in the United States of America

# Contents

## *Feeling all our feelings...*

## *Moving toward wholeness—slowly, surely...*

## *Living peacefully...*

# *In Loving Memory...*

*The comfort of having a friend may be taken away, but not that of having had one.*

*—Seneca*

This little book is dedicated to the memory of my special friend, Alice Felts. In her quiet, unassuming way, she taught me all about love, friendship, kindness and, in the end, courage. Mother Teresa once said, "Give of your hands to serve and your hearts to love." I know of no one whose life was more about serving and loving than Alice's.

I think of her and miss her every day. It was hard to give her up but I did so willingly because I know she is in a better place—whole again and no longer in pain—enfolded in God's arms and surrounded by His perfect love. And I know with all my heart that she is singing with a host of other angels in that glorious Heavenly Choir!

Rest in peace, my dear friend.

# *Preface*

*I have found over the years that my writing has more courage than I do.*

—*Linda Hogan*

For some reason, I have felt compelled to write lately. And I do mean "compelled"—I don't really want to write but I *have* to write. And when I ran across Linda Hogan's wonderful quote, everything came together for me. I must write what is in my heart but I'm afraid of what will emerge. I think I'm afraid the real me will come out in my writing. And I'm not sure if I'm ready to find out who I really am.

At first I was going to write a book—a sort of autobiographical novel, if you will. I wrote the Prologue and it was pretty good. Then I started writing the book and it was garbage! I was so hung up on writing it perfectly the first time—in the right order with exactly the right pen and the right color of ink on the right size paper—it's no wonder the words never came.

Then I realized what I really wanted to do was write about things that are dear to me—a series of meditations as it were—to describe some of the experiences I've had, especially in the last ten years or so since I stopped living in the fog of denial and alcoholism and started seeing the world as it really is. This kind of writing made perfect sense to me because one of my greatest comforts over the years has been a variety of meditation books. I read them every morning and every night. Starting and ending my day with some quiet time keeps me centered and sane.

Because my dog-eared meditation books have meant so much to me over the years, I'm hoping my writings might make a difference in another person's life. I know what I write here won't blaze any new trails in literature or win any Pulitzer prizes, but it comes from my heart and that is why I must write it. Perhaps someone at a difficult place along life's journey will find comfort in something I write—perhaps they will read it and say, "I know exactly how you feel—you must be a mind reader!" And if I can make just one person's burdens a bit lighter, I will not have written in vain.

# A Word of Thanks...

I want to specifically thank Pat Brown for her legal expertise, Curt Yeo for his technical expertise, and Rifka Keilson at iUniverse for her assistance and patience.

In addition, I am grateful to all of you whose lives have touched mine—each one of you played a part in making me the person I am today. I am grateful to my parents, my brother, and my extended family for the love and support they have given me. I am also grateful to my special friends, including my support groups and counselors, for the constant encouragement they have given me and for their belief in me—you all know who you are. And finally, I thank God for having created me as one of His unique children and for the journey—sometimes wondrous and sometimes bumpy—He and I are on together. I can't wait for the next chapter to unfold!

Betty Bennett

# *Before You Start Reading...*

I have a couple of general comments about this book which I want to share with you here. First, I want to explain my use of the words "God" and "Higher Power." I have used them interchangeably throughout. While I believe in God (who is *my* Higher Power), I realize there will be readers who don't share my belief. As you will discover in the "12-Step Programs" section, all recovery work is based upon the premise that you must turn your life over to a "Higher Power of *your own choosing*." It is for this reason that I have used both "Higher Power" and "God" in my book.

Second, each topic is complete in and of itself. You may want to read the book from cover to cover (and I hope you do!), but there may also be times when you want to read about a single topic ("Grief," "Nature," etc.). So if you do read this book from cover to cover, you will find a bit of repetition from time to time. That's because something I've written about one topic may be just as pertinent to other topics. I've tried to keep this repetition to a minimum, but I did want to mention it for all you alert readers out there!

And now—enjoy!!

# Learning to survive...

# Twelve-Step Programs

*The journey of a thousand miles begins with one step.*

*—Lao-tse*

*It is never too late to be what you might have been.*

*—George Eliot*

Ten years ago I didn't know what a 12-step program was. Yes, I had heard of Alcoholics Anonymous (AA)—I knew that's where people went who had a drinking problem, but that was about the extent of my knowledge.

I found out about 12-step programs the hard way. When my marriage and my life were in shambles, I knew I had to do something. Nothing I had tried so far had worked. I had hit rock bottom. Someone encouraged me to go to a 12-step meeting and the rest, as they say, is history.

I started going to two 12-step groups: ACiR (Adult Children in Recovery) and CoDA (Codependents Anonymous). I have to say that going to the first meeting of each of these groups was one of the hardest things I have ever done. I never would have done it if there had been any other way out. I kept telling myself that I could always leave the meeting if it made me too uncomfortable—I was always o.k. as long as I had a "Plan B." Besides, I figured everyone there had been in my shoes when they went to their first meeting and that gave me strength and comfort. And even as green as I was back then, I did realize that going to that first meeting took an incredible amount of courage, so I was very proud of myself. I think that's one of the first times I actually gave myself credit for doing something that took courage (but it was by no means the last!).

Making these two 12-step groups a part of my life was one of the best things I ever did, and attending these meetings every week probably saved my life. In ACiR, I came face to face with my childhood and the role I played as part of a dysfunctional household (and by the way, *all* households are dysfunctional—it's just a matter of degree). With lots of work, I was able to put the past behind me, live in the present, and anticipate the future with joy. At that point, I stopped going to the ACiR meetings.

The CoDA meetings were much more difficult because I had to come to grips with *myself*. No longer could I blame someone or something—I had to work on myself—who I was, what my issues were, and what I wanted to do with the rest of my life. This was much harder than ACiR and it took much longer.

<u>What I Learned</u>

Twelve-step programs are—

- <u>Confidential</u>—nothing you say or hear in a meeting should ever be repeated outside the meeting

- <u>Anonymous</u>—first names only

- <u>Available</u> for anyone who is suffering and wants to recover, regardless of race, sex, age, religious affiliation (or not), economic status, etc. Many times there are specialized 12-step meetings within a particular recovery group (for example, a women's CoDA group or a gay and lesbian AA group)

- <u>Non-judgmental</u>—in all the 12-step meetings I attended, no "cross talk" was allowed. That means you can't respond to or try to "fix" the person who is sharing what's happening in their life. (I must confess there were times when I literally had to sit on my hands to keep from doing this!)

- <u>Voluntary</u>—The usual procedure in these meetings is to go around the room and let anyone share who wants to. If you don't want to share, you simply pass. When I first started going to these meetings, I sat and listened for several weeks until I felt comfortable sharing with the group.

- <u>Free</u>—There is no charge for these meetings, although usually a $1 contribution per meeting is appreciated.

- <u>Healing</u>—There is something very healing and "normalizing" about attending these meetings. You realize you aren't the only one with problems (many times, people in recovery share similar problems) and you come to realize you aren't alone or crazy. In fact, going to a meeting and talking about your situation is probably one of the sanest things you can do!

The first three steps of all 12-step programs set the tone for the next nine. They are paraphrased below:

1. Admitted we were powerless over (alcohol, drugs, sex, food, etc.)—our lives were out of control.

2. Realized that a Power greater than ourselves could help us.

3. Decided to turn our will and our lives over to God, or the Higher Power of our choosing.

For this program to work, you have to admit that you are powerless over your addiction, that your life is out of control, and that a Power greater than yourself can make you sane again—then you must make a commitment to turn your life over to the care of your Higher Power. I was able to "work" Steps 1 and 2 pretty easily—I knew I was powerless and that my life was a mess (Step 1) and I did believe in God and believed He could do for me what I couldn't do for myself (Step 2). My problem came with Step 3—having to turn my life over to God. I was a control freak and turning anything over to anybody was very hard for me. It took a long time for me to come to terms with this step and actually work it. In fact, I continue to work it many times each day.

I want to make special mention of the terms, "Power greater than ourselves" and "God." Twelve-step programs are deeply spiritual but they are not religious. However, it is essential for us to believe that some "Higher Power" of our choosing is in control of our lives and that we are not.

Background and General Information

I was amazed to find out how many 12-step programs there are! In addition to AA, here are a few more:

- Al-Anon—for families and friends of alcoholics

- Alateen—for young Al-Anon members, usually teenagers, whose lives have been affected by someone else's drinking

- Adult Children of Alcoholics (ACoA)—for adults who were children in alcoholic or other dysfunctional families

- Co-Dependents Anonymous (CoDA)—for those whose common purpose is to develop healthy relationships

- Gamblers Anonymous (GA)—for those recovering from a gambling addiction

- Narcotics Anonymous (NA)—for those recovering from drug addiction

- Nar-Anon—for families and friends of drug addicts

- Overeaters Anonymous (OA)—for those recovering from compulsive overeating

And that's only the tip of the iceberg. When I accessed the Google search engine recently and entered "12-step programs," it gave me 47,600 sites! And one site alone listed 136 different 12-step groups. All of them reach out to addicts—people whose lives are controlled by a substance or an action.

All 12-step programs have their roots in Alcoholics Anonymous which was founded in 1935 by Bill W., a New York stockbroker, and Dr. Bob S., an Akron, OH, surgeon—both of whom were hopeless alcoholics. Bill W. wrote the 12 Steps of AA to summarize its recovery program.

(For a truthful and poignant portrayal of the beginning of AA and the struggles Bill W. and Dr. Bob S. had with alcoholism, I highly recommend the video "My Name is Bill W." starring James Woods and James Garner. Two other excellent movies dealing realistically with alcoholism are "The Verdict" starring Paul Newman and "Leaving Las Vegas" starring Nicholas Cage. Both movies are brutally honest in their portrayal of alcoholism. Finally, Sen. George McGovern has written a beautiful and deeply moving book about his daughter and her struggles with alcohol, which eventually killed her. It is called, simply, *Terry*.)

# Serenity Prayer

*God, grant me the serenity to accept the things I cannot change;*
*the courage to change the things I can;*
*and the wisdom to know the difference.*

—*Serenity Prayer from Alcoholics Anonymous*

*God, give us the grace to accept with serenity the things that cannot be*
*changed, courage to change the things which should be changed, and the wis-*
*dom to distinguish the one from the other.*

—*Reinhold Niebuhr*

I must have repeated this prayer a hundred times in 12-step meetings before it really sank in. What a simple but powerful prayer! If we could apply it to every situation we face, what a difference it would make in our lives.

<u>Accept the things I cannot change</u>—Think about all the situations we face every day—at work, at home, in relationships with family and friends. How many of them are beyond our control? Can we really change a spouse who drinks or a boss who verbally abuses us? The answer is "no." We can take care of ourselves and we can choose to remove ourselves from an unhealthy situation (especially if we are the victim of any kind of abuse), but the only person we can change is ourselves and the only way we can influence others is to set an example by the way we live our life.

If we follow the Serenity Prayer, what must we do? When we cannot change something—or someone—we must "let go (in love) and let God." We must turn the person or situation over to God in love and *let it go*. Is this hard? You bet it is! But you know what? Once we do it—*really* do it, both intellectually and emotionally—it is such a relief. A huge burden is taken off our shoulders and in its place come feelings of peace and serenity. Isn't it freeing to know we're not in charge of everything? That we can turn it over to God and let Him take care of it? What a relief!

<u>Change the things I can</u>—The fourth step of all 12-step programs often stops a lot of people in recovery dead in their tracks because it says you must make a fearless and searching moral inventory of yourself! It is one of the pivotal 12 steps because it forces you to come face to face with yourself. What are the things you like about yourself? What are the things you would like to change?

When I was first introduced to this step, I knew I wouldn't have any problem listing all my negative traits but I was hard-pressed to think of anything positive about myself. How very sad. Because an inventory is really about who we are and what we think about ourselves at a particular time. And at any given time, there should be qualities about ourselves that we like as well as those we want to work on.

In fact, one of the first things I knew I needed to change was to stop being so hard on myself. I was my own worst enemy and no matter what I did or how well I did it, it never measured up to my high standards. I came to realize I was a perfectionist and that nothing I did would ever meet those standards. So I embarked on a wondrous journey of self-discovery and self-love. I have learned to give myself some slack—I'm doing the best I can, and that's good enough! I started taking care of myself physically and emotionally. Inch by inch, as I continued to work on my inventory, I came to realize I had many positive traits—I wasn't such a "bad" person after all! And I know now that until I came to love and respect myself, I could not begin to love and respect others. Make no mistake about it—taking care of ourselves is not selfish—it is *essential* to our good mental, physical, and emotional health.

As far as my perfectionism goes, well, let's just say that I'm making progress and, like most issues in my life, I work on it one day at a time

If we're completely honest when we make our inventory, we will begin to see some qualities that we would like to work on—some things we want to change. These could involve character traits or relationships. Are we quick to anger and snap at our kids? Perhaps we need to figure out why we're so angry, work through it, and move on. Are we in a relationship with someone who is an active addict? Perhaps we need to get out. Getting out is something we can change; changing the addict is not.

It takes courage to make a fearless and searching moral inventory of ourselves and to work on changing the things we can.

<u>The wisdom to know the difference</u>—Without question, this is the most powerful—and the hardest—part of this prayer. Every day I pray for the wisdom to

deal with the situations life throws at me that day. Is it something that needs to be changed and that I can change? If so, I ask God for the courage to change it. Is it something that I can't change, no matter how much I want to or think it needs to be changed? If so, I ask God to help me let it go in love. But most importantly, I pray for the wisdom to know the difference.

# *Codependency*

*Definition:* *Those self-defeating, learned behaviors or character defects that result in a diminished capacity to initiate or to participate in loving relationships.*

—*Earnie Larsen*

*What's a codependent? The answer's easy. They're some of the most loving, caring people I know.*

—*Lonny Owen*

Countless books have been written about codependency since it became a buzz word among mental health professionals in the late seventies. The two books that helped me most (and changed my life) are both by Melody Beattie: *Codependent No More* and *Beyond Codependency*. For me, Beattie captured the essence of codependency in the subtitle to *Codependent No More*: "How to Stop Controlling Others and Start Caring for Yourself."

When I first started going to CoDA meetings, like all newcomers I kept asking, "What is codependency?" and "How do I know if I'm codependent?" (Some part of me still desperately wanted to believe that everything was o.k. and that I wasn't "crazy.")

At my CoDA meetings, I quickly learned that Melody Beattie is considered to be the "guru" of the codependency movement. I was told there was a list of characteristics describing this addiction in *Codependent No More* which would help me decide whether or not I was codependent.

I bought her book and started reading. I couldn't put it down. The person she kept describing was *me*! How did she know? After I had underlined at least three-fourths of the first few chapters, I knew that I was extremely codependent and that I had a lot of work ahead of me.

There are many characteristics that describe codependent behavior. Here are a few, excerpted from *Codependent No More*:

Codependents—

- reject compliments or praise

- can't make a decision

- fear rejection

- fear making a mistake

- want to do everything perfectly

- don't think anyone could like/love them

- worry, worry, WORRY

- wonder why they can't get things done

- think things will be better tomorrow

- are compulsive spenders, eaters, workaholics—you fill in the blank

- think they are going crazy

I found these two books to be very readable and believable, and it's because Beattie knows what's she's talking about. She is a recovering alcoholic and drug addict. She had been in recovery for both of these addictions for some time when she realized things still weren't "right" in her life. This baffled her because she was making great progress in recovering from her addictions. It was then that she started to do some serious research on codependency.

She came to believe that codependency is an addiction that is a part of all other addictions. In other words, alcoholics are codependent, drug addicts are codependent, etc. In fact, it's often because of the root addiction (alcoholism, for example) that addicts and people involved with addicts become codependent.

Let me take you inside a house where an alcoholic lives. In this household, everyone has a role to play, although those involved may not even realize this. The alcoholic, quite obviously, drinks! Other family members become caretakers. Children are often thrust into the role of being the intermediary, or referee, between the alcoholic and his/her spouse.

And throughout the household, telltale signs of codependency begin to emerge: stuffing our feelings, never discussing what's really going on (the "elephant in the living room" syndrome), walking on eggshells, bargaining (promising to do anything if the alcoholic will just stop drinking), thinking it's our fault the person started drinking or continues to drink, and trying to remain invisible so we won't become the object of the alcoholic's bizarre behavior.

In addition to developing these codependent behaviors, family members constantly live with fear because they never know when the alcoholic might exhibit irrational, erratic, and often dangerous behavior. All they know is that it *will* happen.

I want to make one point very clear: all of us on this planet are codependent to some degree, and that's normal and healthy. Not one of us could survive for long without interacting with other people. Besides, who would want to?

There are, however, degrees of codependency just as there are degrees of dysfunctionality (which go hand in hand, by the way). When you have lost your own identity and no longer know who you are; when you take care of everyone but yourself; when you keep thinking things will be better tomorrow (and they never are); when you feel like a slug moving in a million different directions trying to please everyone but yourself; when you depend on other people or your possessions to make your life complete and bring you happiness—*then* you have crossed the line and become a codependent.

Yes, as one of the quotes above says, codependents are some of the most caring, loving people around. It's just that we spend so much time taking care of others that we have no time left for ourselves. We always put our wants and needs last. Perhaps one reason we do this is that as long as we're taking care of everyone else, we don't have to come face to face with ourselves. It's always easier to tell others what they should be doing than work on our own issues, isn't it? It's easy to "fix" others—we just can't seem to "fix" ourselves.

So how do you go about working on this addiction? Here are a few suggestions that worked for me:

- Get yourself to a CoDA 12-step meeting

- Select a friend you can talk to confidentially who won't judge you or tell you what to do, and start sharing your feelings (it will be hard at first but it really does get easier)

- Buy—or get from the library—some self-help books on codependency and start reading them

- Start keeping a journal—writing is a wonderful way to express your feelings

• Do something nice for yourself every day—whether it's giving yourself a compliment, treating yourself to a massage, or going to a movie—get used to taking care of *you*

In the pages that follow, I will discuss some of the behaviors we codependents often struggle with on a daily basis.

# Assertiveness

*All the mistakes I ever made in my life were when I wanted to say no and said yes.*

—*Moss Hart*

*We need to find the courage to say NO to the things and people that are not serving us if we want to rediscover ourselves and live our lives with authenticity.*

—*Barbara de Angelis*

The issue I struggle with most—many times each day, in fact—is how to be assertive. Why? Because it affects everything I do in every aspect of my life.

We basically deal with all relationship situations in one of three ways—passively, aggressively, or assertively. Passive behavior moves against ourselves and aggressive behavior moves against others. If we act passively, we go out of our way to roll over and play dead in order to avoid a confrontation or make someone angry. If we act aggressively, we take our anger and frustration out on others. When we act assertively, we respect both the other person *and* ourselves.

In their excellent book, *Speaking the Truth in Love*, Ruth N. Koch and Kenneth G. Haugk say that assertiveness "is behavior that honors the self while honoring others." What a wonderful, concise definition! It sounds so simple—why is it so hard?

Speaking the truth isn't usually too difficult, it's speaking the truth *in love* that's the hard part. How can we honor ourselves and honor others at the same time? Here are some things I've learned about being assertive over the years:

- Being assertive affects every relationship we have, including those at work, with family, with friends, and with a significant other.

- We can be assertive in one relationship and not in another—for example, we can be assertive at work but not in situations involving family or friends. I have always found it most difficult to assert myself in family situations.

- You and I might handle the same situation differently. You might not have a problem assertively standing up to your boss, while I might passively do nothing or aggressively take my feelings out on my dogs.

- We could respond to the same situation differently at different times, depending on what kind of mood we're in, how important it is to us, etc.

Now here's where it gets interesting! Did you know you can demonstrate passive or aggressive behavior and still be assertive? Did you know you can say nothing and still be assertive? How is this possible?

The key to being assertive is that *you are in charge*. In any given situation, you can choose to be passive, aggressive, or assertive. We must assess each situation and decide if it's important enough for us to tackle or if doing so would be in our best interests. We may be frustrated with a situation at work but if being assertive means we're likely to lose our job, we have to decide if it's worth the risk.

<u>NOTE:</u> We do not *ever* have to accept any form of abuse, whether it's physical, verbal, or emotional.

We must be willing to accept the consequences of our assertive behavior. Being assertive involves taking a risk because we don't know how the other person will react.

Here are some tips on how to be more assertive:

- Buy yourself some time if you can. If someone asks me to do something, no matter how tempting it sounds, I have learned to say, "Let me think about it and get back to you." That way I can take my time making a decision.

- Once you have made your decision, tell the other person. Be succinct and firm. You don't have to explain, or apologize for, your decision nor do you have to give detailed explanations or excuses (this only weakens your answer).

- If you'll be talking on the phone, consider writing your message out before making the call. That way, you'll cover all your points and you won't veer off course.

- If you must respond immediately, take several deep breaths first.

It's not easy to speak the truth in love. It takes patience, honesty, understanding, and love. I can give you many examples of times when I did speak the truth in love and other times when I didn't even come close. But I keep trying because when it happens—when I've respected both the other person and myself—it's an absolutely wonderful feeling!

# *Boundaries*

*Boundaries are personal property lines that define who you are and who you are not, and influence all areas of your life.*

—Drs. Henry Cloud and John Townsend, <u>Boundaries</u>

*I decided to do more*
*of what I wanted to do,*
*stopped doing many things*
*I didn't want to do, and*
*gave up worrying about those*
*things I had no control over.*

—*Anon.*

I had no idea what it meant to set a boundary until recently. I spent most of my life trying to fit in with others—trying to please them so they would like me—or at the very least, hoping to fade into the woodwork so I wouldn't stick out like a sore thumb. Sometimes I think I had more personalities than Sybil!

As I think back on my life, I realize that I was a lot like an amoeba—you know, one of those one-celled organisms that slowly oozes in this direction and that like a shapeless blob. I rarely had a thought of my own. If people wanted to go out to eat, I would tell them anywhere they wanted to go was fine with me. Same goes for a picking a movie. Or deciding what to fix for dinner.

I remember someone once asked me what my favorite color was, and I was appalled to realize that I had no idea! How very sad. (I'm happy to tell you now that it's *blue!*)

In their book, *Boundaries*, Drs. Cloud and Townsend ask what the first and most basic boundary is for all of us—I was surprised to learn that it is our skin. They go on to say that the skin does what all good boundaries do: it keeps the good things in (like our bones and organs) and it keeps the bad things out (like germs and infection). When I think about it, I can't think of a better or simpler definition of boundaries than that: they keep the good things in and the bad things out. Simple definition—but hard to live by!

The authors also point out that a boundary isn't a wall we create between ourselves and others; rather, it's more like a fence with a gate that we can open or shut as we set boundaries with others.

As the quote above says, boundaries define who we are and who we aren't. And they definitely affect every aspect of our lives. The paradox about boundaries is that although they are sometimes hard to set, once we set them our lives become much easier. We are free to do the things we *really* want to do, rather than the things others want us to do—or the things we *think* others want us to do.

Setting a boundary involves taking a risk because you can't predict how the other person will respond. You have to be willing to accept the consequences of setting a boundary because:

> *The most important part about setting a boundary*
> *is that you must commit to keep it once you set it.*

Here are some ways to set boundaries:

Say "No"

You've probably seen the saying on t-shirts and coffee mugs that says, "What part of 'NO' don't you understand?" What a great question. Why is it so hard for us to say "no"? Are we afraid the other person won't like us or will get angry with us if we turn them down? Do we honestly think we can do everything we are asked to do—and do it all well? Or are we allowing ourselves to be "dumped on" because we enjoy being a martyr? Whatever our reason, saying "yes" to everything we're asked to do can have a disastrous effect on our lives and our health.

There may be times when it's harder to say "no" than others. I have a hard time saying "no" when I'm asked to do something for my church. Why? Because I know it's always for a good cause and I feel guilty when I decline. I need to get over that! I'm not doing the project or myself any good if I agree to do something I don't have time for or I'm not interested in.

I must learn to start saying "no"—so I can begin to:

Say "Yes"

Being able to say "no" when I don't want to do something frees me up to start saying "yes" to the things I enjoy. It's all about putting myself first—finding out who I really am, what my interests are, what I'm passionate about—and getting on with the business of doing the things that are important to me and that bring me joy.

Sometimes we also need to be able to:

## Say When

I once set a boundary with someone and he agreed to do what I asked him. However, he kept dragging his feet and postponing it. It was then I realized I should have asked him to do what I had asked him to do by a specific, realistic date (which I later did). That's the other part about setting a boundary—often we must include a "due date" and be prepared to enforce our boundary after that date.

◆       ◆       ◆

Saying "no"—saying "yes"—saying when—we can use all these tools to help us set boundaries so we can live our lives to the fullest, doing the things that interest, challenge, and fulfill us.

# Detaching in Love

*If you aren't good at loving yourself, you will have a difficult time loving anyone, since you'll resent the time and energy you give another person that you aren't even giving to yourself.*

—*Barbara de Angelis*

Detachment is a term that is often used in recovery. I suppose you could think of detachment as being a defense mechanism, but detaching in love is a healthy solution to many relationship issues.

One of the biggest problems we codependents have is getting involved with other folks' issues. We're just sure we know what someone else should do to solve a particular problem, and we're not at all shy about dispensing our advice! In fact, we often get so involved in other people's issues that we take them on as our own. We're totally incapable of setting a boundary between ourselves and the other person.

Why do we do this? It could be because we're very caring people with a genuine desire to help other people. It could also be because it's easier for us to solve other people's problems than it is to work on our own. Most codependents put themselves at the very bottom of the list of people to take care of. If they work long enough and hard enough trying to solve everyone else's problems, they may never have to come face to face with their own.

There may come a time in our lives when we must detach from someone we love. This is usually very difficult and painful. Why would we need to detach? If someone we love is an active addict, for example, we need to remove ourselves from this person's life. We can't make that person stop actively using—only the addict can make that decision. But we absolutely do *not* have to remain in the life of an active addict. It is detrimental to our emotional, and sometimes our physical, health.

We may also need to detach from a family member or members when their behavior is adversely affecting us. Depending on the circumstances, this detachment could be temporary or permanent. We might have to remove ourselves physically from this person—perhaps even go so far as to move to another geographical location. The important thing is to take care of ourselves and to detach in love from unhealthy relationships.

So how do we go about detaching in love? One definition of "detached" in *Webster's II New College Dictionary* is "free from emotional, intellectual, or social involvement." That is exactly what we need to do—free ourselves from involvement in the problems of others. That doesn't mean we can't care for and be concerned about these people and the issues they're facing. It doesn't mean we can't empathize with them and be there for them when they need a shoulder to cry on. It *does* mean we can't try to fix their problems ourselves or tell them what they should do.

Detaching in love is about removing ourselves from situations we have no control over and shouldn't be involved in anyway. It's about setting a boundary between us and the other person and sticking to it. It's about loving and honoring ourselves and the other person enough to let that person go in love to solve whatever problem he or she is facing.

When we use detachment this way, it is not a defense mechanism, it is a healthy way to take care of ourselves.

# *Perfectionism*

*Striving for excellence motivates you; striving for perfection is demoralizing.*

—*Harriet Braiker*

*Perfectionism does not exist; to understand it is the triumph of human intelligence; to expect to possess it is the most dangerous kind of madness.*

—*Alfred de Musset*

It is absolutely true that striving for perfection is both demoralizing and a kind of madness. What's more, perfection cannot be achieved. I wish I had known and believed that years ago—I could have saved myself many hours of anguish.

Those of us who strive for perfection are strange birds and we often come with lots of baggage. Many of us grew up in a home where an addiction existed. Many of us consciously or unconsciously blamed ourselves for the person's addiction. Quite mistakenly, we thought *we* were the cause of the addiction. We convinced ourselves it was something we did or said. So, in our ignorance, what solutions did we come up with? We needed to be smarter, prettier, thinner, quieter—well, you get the picture. We needed to be perfect!

It took me years to realize that even if I *had* been perfect (and God knows I tried!), it wouldn't have made any difference in the life of the addict. Only the addict can change the addict.

I distinctly remember coming home from junior-high school one day with all A's on my report card, except for one A-. The feedback I got was that an A- wasn't good enough and I needed to work hard to bring that up to at least an A by the end of the next grading period. Is it any wonder that, to this day, I continue to grade myself and my life? ("I didn't do a very good job standing up for myself today—I would give myself a C-.") I actually said something similar to this in a 12-step meeting one night and a very wise person said to me, "You're not in school any more."!

This pattern of striving for perfection was part of my marriage too. I particularly remember the planning we put into a large sit-down dinner we were having.

We literally spent hours coming up with the "perfect," politically correct seating arrangement for a diverse group of people, some of whom didn't like each other. All our work came tumbling down the minute everyone found their places around the tables. One unknowing soul went to her assigned seat, picked up her place card and moved somewhere else—it seems she was left-handed and she didn't like where we had put her. So much for the "perfect" seating arrangement! I thought both my husband and I would have apoplexy—the dinner was ruined for us before it even began.

My therapist once asked me if it would be hard for me to stop trying to be perfect. I said I didn't think it would be too hard—in fact, given all the other difficult issues I was working on at that time, I thought that would be the easiest one to tackle—and conquer. I was wrong!! It's one of the hardest things I've ever had to do, and I still struggle with it every day.

One lesson I have learned is to "know your audience." If I'm sending e-mail to a group of co-workers, it doesn't have to be nearly as "perfect" as a letter to a client would need to be.

There's a fine line between doing the best you can and letting it go, and trying to do everything perfectly. But think about it—if you perform at a 95-percent accuracy level, isn't that good enough? Isn't it a waste of your time and energy to try to reach the 100-percent accuracy level, especially when you know that isn't possible?

I will warn you that trying *not* to be perfect will be painfully difficult, especially in the beginning. But it does get easier with practice. And remember this—if we're performing at a 95-percent accuracy level, we're out-performing almost everyone else on the planet!

# *Procrastination*

*How lovely to think that no one need wait a moment, we can start now, start slowly changing the world!*

—*Anne Frank*

*Begin doing what you want to do now. We are not living in eternity. We have only this moment, sparkling like a star in our hand—and melting like a snowflake. Let us use it before it is too late.*

—*Marie Beyon Ray*

I am a big procrastinator. It seems I stay overwhelmed all the time and because there's so much for me to do, I don't do anything. That just doubles my trouble. First of all, I'm not getting anything accomplished and second, the list of things I have to do gets longer and longer. I'm constantly adding to my to-do list instead of checking things off. Which means I feel more and more overwhelmed every day.

What makes my procrastination even worse is that I know better. Intellectually I know that if I complete a couple of projects each day or spend a certain amount of time regularly working on my to-do list, I'll feel better because I can start to check things off. And once I force myself to get started, I always feel better. It's just that most of the time I can't seem to get started.

Why is that? Since I often sit on my sofa doing nothing, I've had a lot of time to mull this over! Here are some thoughts I came up with as they relate to a major procrastination of mine, clearing out all the junk in my house:

- Being a perfectionist, I think I have to do this job perfectly or not at all. Even when I get inspired to do something (or, more honestly, when things get so bad that even I can't tolerate them any longer), after I've made piles of things to keep and things to discard, I always end up with a third pile of stuff I don't know what to do with. So it usually goes back in a shopping bag to be dealt with the next time I force myself to clean up.

- The sheer volume of what I need to do overwhelms me. It seems that everywhere I look, something needs to be done. I usually follow the path of least resistance and sit on my sofa working crossword puzzles instead. Here's an example: I couldn't find something I really needed recently and after much searching I found it, quite by accident, in one of my kitchen drawers. The drawer was in such awful shape that I decided I couldn't stand it another minute so I cleaned it out. It took about 15 minutes and most everything in the drawer ended up in the trashcan! I felt so good afterward—the drawer looked great and it hadn't taken me very long to accomplish that task. That's the up side. The down side is that there are many other drawers in my kitchen that also need to be cleaned out, then there are junky drawers in other rooms, then there are lots of cabinets that need help—well, you get the picture. I am completely overwhelmed.

- Some of the stuff I need to sort through would be painful for me to deal with. This is especially true when I start looking at things of my mother's (who died several years ago) or things that were part of my life when I was married (which ended in divorce a number of years ago). I know I avoid dealing with sentimental things because of the memories they will evoke.

- Maybe one of my fears is that I actually *will* finish this project—and then what will I do? Could it be that I keep putting off this mammoth task because I don't want to look beyond it to find the real me? There's a wonderful book by Julie Morgenstern called *Organizing from the Inside Out* and it really speaks to me. I believe the clutter in my house is directly related to the clutter in my mind and maybe I don't want to clear either of them out. As long as I don't finish this project, I have the perfect excuse for not moving on to other projects—in a very real way it's my "ace in the hole."

- When I'm really honest with myself, I must admit that I'm rebelling against the structure and order that was prevalent in my marriage. We had lists for everything—menus for all our meals, Christmas gifts we gave and received every year, detailed lists about every dinner party we ever gave (and there were quite a few!), including the menu, who was there, what my husband and I wore, etc. It's no wonder that I don't like to be organized any more—even though I have to admit the pendulum has swung too far in the other direction!

- Maybe I'm just lazy! I don't like to do housework—I never have. Since I live alone now, I think I have convinced myself that I can be a slob if I want to—who's going to stop me?

Most likely, the answer to my puzzling problem is that it's a combination of all of the above. You know what I wish? I wish I could start off even—not have to deal with all the mess I've got now—just start with everything being neat and tidy and see if I can keep it that way. The problem is that the only way for me to wipe the slate clean and start again from scratch is to tackle and complete my most dreaded project.

# Self-Esteem

*No one can make you feel inferior without your consent.*

*—Eleanor Roosevelt*

*But if I tell you who I am, you may not like who I am, and it is all that I have.*

*—John Powell, <u>Why Am I Afraid to Tell You Who I Am?</u>*

Since I am a perfectionist (although I'm working on that!), I have suffered from low self-esteem most of my life. Think about it—when you're convinced you have to do everything perfectly and the reality is that you can't possibly succeed, you're going to be disappointed over and over again. Not achieving our goals (however rigid and unattainable they may be) is a major cause of low self-esteem.

Living in a household where an addiction is present also affects how we feel about ourselves. We're trying so hard to be the perfect child or the perfect spouse, walking on eggshells so we won't upset the addict, that it's no wonder we suppress who we really are.

Low self-esteem often manifests itself in the work place in the guise of being passed over for a promotion, being laid off, etc. I once had someone tell me, "Don't take it personally" and I wanted to say to him, "Wait until it happens to you and then tell me not to take it personally." I have seen first-hand the devastation losing a job (and the inability to get another one) can cause.

My already fragile self-esteem suffered another blow when my ex-husband and I separated. I saw this separation as the most public kind of humiliation. Now the whole world would know I was a failure as a wife and everyone would pity me.

What did I do? What most introverts do, I suppose. I created a wall around me that no one could penetrate. Except for going to work, I stayed home with my dogs, eating and watching TV. I convinced myself that I was completely unlovable. In retrospect, I know I built that wall around me because I didn't want anyone to get close enough to ever hurt me again. So as long as I stayed home and ate all the ice cream I could get my hands on, I was safe from the world. So what if I gained a lot of weight? What difference did it make? I hated myself and I was not about to let anyone else into my life. Besides, the ice cream tasted good!

All of which brings me to the crux of the issue of self-esteem: *self-esteem is directly proportional to self-love.* The first step toward feeling good about ourselves is learning to love ourselves and becoming comfortable with who we are.

How did I—and do I—go about this? Oh boy, I wish I could tell you I read a couple of self-help books and woke up one morning feeling "all better." NOT!! It was a slow and often painful process and it is ongoing even as I write.

At some point, I realized that self-esteem is also closely related to vulnerability. When we're at a bad place in our lives (for example, my separation and divorce), we often close ourselves off because we don't want to be vulnerable. Why should we let anyone else hurt us? Haven't we been hurt enough already? How much pain can one person take anyhow?

Attending 12-step programs helped me work on my self-esteem. One of the steps is to prepare a self-inventory, and as I worked on my inventory I realized I had character *assets* as well as defects, even though it took me a while to come up with any of my assets.

Another turning point was when I decided I wanted to lose some weight so that I would feel better about myself. I started working with a nutritionist/therapist so I could lose weight healthily. I realized at the time that I was taking a huge step because I was letting the wall I had built around me start to crumble—I was starting to let myself become vulnerable again. It was very scary and it still is at times.

What I keep telling myself over and over again is that I'm good enough just the way I am right now, and I'm beginning to like myself a bit better. I know I can't control what other people think of me—all I can do is live my life so that it pleases me.

There's a great Ricky Nelson oldie-goldie called "Garden Party" and one of the lines goes something like, "I can't please everyone, so I have to please myself." That says it all!

# Surviving the Holidays and Other Tough Times

*People are like stained glass windows. They sparkle and shine when the sun is out, but when the darkness sets in, their true beauty is revealed only if there is a light from within.*

—*Elisabeth Kübler-Ross*

*Often God has to shut a door in our face, so that He can subsequently open the door through which He wants us to go.*

—*Catharine Marshall*

I would be willing to bet that there are as many people who are miserable during the holidays as there are ones who are happy. In fact, I'll bet there are more who are miserable. And I'm convinced that some of the ones who seem to be happy are living in a fog of denial or are using drugs or alcohol (or both) to get them through.

Thanksgiving and Christmas were always special to me. A lot of my family lived in the same town and we spent all our holidays together. So my childhood memories of those times are very happy ones—I remember them as being filled with laughter and fellowship and good food.

In recent years, however, the holidays have become quite different—and often difficult—for me. My family doesn't live close by any more and many of them have died over the years. So those fun-filled holiday gatherings are just distant memories now.

I have spent Thanksgiving Day alone more than once in the last few years, and I didn't like it. Those were times when I was both alone *and* lonely. Childhood memories of Thanksgivings past flooded my mind and filled me with sadness. Why couldn't things be the way they used to be? Why did I have to be so sad and so alone?

But for me, spending Thanksgiving Day alone paled in comparison to coping with the Christmas season. After all, Thanksgiving is just one day and I have learned to live life one day at a time, secure in the knowledge that I can make it through that day. Besides, I know I can always go shopping the day after Thanksgiving!

The Christmas season, on the other hand, is not just one day. Thanks to the "wonderful" folks in the retail industry(!), it starts long before Thanksgiving and lasts until after New Year's. And there's no way I can ignore it unless I wrap myself in a soundproof plastic bubble or move to the moon! I completely understand it when people who are sad tell me they wish they could just go to sleep before Thanksgiving and wake up sometime after New Year's. Sounds good to me!

Why are the holidays so difficult for a lot of us? There are usually several reasons. One of them is that we assume everyone else is having a wonderful holiday. This is the classic example of comparing our insides to others' outsides. We look at other people who *seem* to be happy and we yearn to be like them.

Another reason we sometimes have trouble getting through the holidays is that we buy into all the media hype that bombards us this time of year, especially TV ads. You know the ones I'm talking about: the whole family sitting around the dining room table smiling and looking perfect while Dad carves the beautifully cooked turkey; the whole family sitting around the beautifully decorated Christmas tree in their Sunday-go-to-meeting finery as they open their beautifully wrapped gifts; the handsome young man giving a diamond necklace (or earrings or bracelet or ring) to his equally beautiful young sweetheart while snow gently falls and soft Christmas music plays in the background.

You know what? I'm getting depressed just writing about these ads! What happens when we see them over and over and over again? We think we should be just like the people in the ad, or we wish we could be just like them, and we know we're not. And since the difference between fantasy and reality is depression, we understandably become depressed.

I want to tell you something: John Boy and the Waltons don't exist and the Christmas cards we receive with those lovely, sometimes poignant, scenes on them are just Christmas cards!

Another reason we struggle during the holidays is that they often evoke "triggers," which are intense feelings of sadness. These triggers often pop up when we least expect them and they come in many forms: the familiar strains of a favorite Christmas carol, a certain scent hanging in the air as we walk through a beautifully decorated department store, or running into someone we knew long ago and haven't seen in ages.

I usually have several "sinking spells" during the holiday season. I can always gauge my emotional stability by whether or not I can listen to Christmas carols. When I'm in a funk, the Christmas carols are the first thing to go—they simply bring up too many memories of Christmases past.

What are some of the reasons the holidays could make us sad? There are many, including losing a loved one, losing a job, moving to a new city, ending a special relationship, getting caught up in the craziness of the holidays, trying to get through them with no crutches (alcohol, drugs, etc.) and, most importantly, not taking care of ourselves physically, emotionally, and spiritually.

So what are some of the things we can do to take care of ourselves during the holidays? The first thing we need to realize is that we might need to get back to basics. Sometimes the best we can hope for is to survive a particularly difficult time, and it is incumbent upon us to do whatever we have to do in order to survive. This may mean making some difficult choices, such as not going home for the holidays, or establishing new traditions if our old ones make us sad. These choices may not please everyone but the important thing is that we take care of ourselves in a healthy way.

We can also be pro-active and find something useful we can do during this time. There's nothing better to take our minds off ourselves and our problems than to reach out to others. Get yourself to a nursing home or a soup kitchen and brighten someone else's life. You'll be surprised by how much brighter *your* life will be as well.

I sometimes wonder why I had to spend some Christmases alone. I have come to the conclusion that one of the reasons is so I can be more aware of, and sympathetic to, the needs of others. Once you've been there yourself, it's not much of a stretch to understand what others are going through. So I try to pay special attention to those I know might be having a difficult holiday. You'd be surprised how much it means to someone to receive a note or a phone call or, even better, an invitation to a Christmas Eve or Christmas Day gathering. Don't ever assume that person has plans—always ask. And don't wait for that person to invite him/herself—take it upon yourself to do the inviting.

There are other trigger times for most people during the year and I try to be mindful of them as well. Those times might include birthdays, wedding anniversaries, anniversaries of the death of a loved one, and any special holidays that could be difficult for someone (Valentine's Day, Mother's Day, Father's Day, etc.). Again, a phone call or a card can go a long way in helping ease that pain.

Don't make the mistake of thinking it would be better not to remind the person of the occasion because it will make them sad—believe me, that's all they're thinking about! Remember—when you reach out in love, you are giving a priceless gift.

# Connecting with a Higher Power…

# Faith and Fear

*A perfect faith would lift us absolutely above fear.*

—*George McDonald*

*I believe in the sun—even when it does not shine; I believe in love—even when it is not shown; I believe in God—even when he does not speak.*

—*Anon.*

Faith and fear are exact opposites. It takes great courage to have faith because we must believe in what we cannot see. Faith is all about believing in something or someone greater than ourselves—a Higher Power of our choice. It's about letting go of our controlling ways and believing that our Higher Power loves us unconditionally and wants only the best for us. It's about letting go of our need to control others, realizing that they have to help themselves and that the only person we're responsible for is ourselves. It's about doing the best we can in any given situation and then letting it go. Most importantly, it's about trust—trust that we are special and unique in the eyes of our Higher Power, who is constantly working to create a life for us that is far richer and more wonderful than we, in our humanness, could ever imagine.

Fear, on the other hand, can take control of our lives and keep us from experiencing so many things. For example, after flying practically all over the world for many years, I suddenly became terrified to fly again, so much so that I would become physically ill just thinking about getting on a plane. This went on for 14 years and although intellectually I realized how much I was missing out on because of my fear, emotionally I was unable to do anything about it. Then, through a series of circumstances (including reading a book about people who are afraid to fly and listening to some encouraging and calming words from a friend who is a private pilot), I got up enough courage to fly again. Getting on a plane for the first time in 14 years was one of the hardest things I've ever done, but *I did it!* It was one of those defining moments in my life when I faced my fear and went through it in spite of the fear. When the plane landed, I was still on Cloud 9!

Procrastination is one of the by-products of fear. Many times I sit around and do nothing—procrastinate—because I'm afraid to try something new or different. It's so much easier to ignore the fear than to recognize it and work through it.

I work every day to conquer my fears and move toward a life filled with faith, love, hope, trust, and joy. Just like everything else, I know I must do it one day at a time.

# *Forgiveness*

*"I can forgive, but I cannot forget," is only another way of saying, "I cannot forgive."*

—*Henry Ward Beecher*

*As long as you don't forgive, who and whatever it is will occupy a rent-free space in your mind.*

—*Isabelle Holland*

Forgiveness is such a key ingredient to a happy life. One version of the Lord's Prayer says, "...forgive us our debts, as we also have forgiven our debtors." (Matthew 6:12, *NIV*) One of the steps in all 12-step programs is about making amends and moving on, and making amends includes forgiveness.

For me, forgiving and forgetting are not easy. Those years I spent in a fog were filled with anger and resentment and vindictiveness. I wanted to lash out at anyone and everyone who was making my life so miserable. I *had* to find someone to blame other than myself. And I did. On any given day, it might be the crazy driver in front of me, or the slowpoke in line ahead of me at the bank, or the co-worker whose cheerful attitude was in such contrast to mine. These people never knew it but they didn't stand a chance. They, along with others too numerous to count, were the recipients of my anger over and over again because I had to have someone to blame.

What I've come to learn in recent years is that forgiveness isn't just about the other person, it's about me as well. Because when I forgive and forget, I set myself free. In many cases, the person we need to forgive doesn't know how we feel about them. For instance, when there is a painful divorce, one spouse might stay angry at the other spouse for years. Most likely, the object of that anger has moved on with his or her life and has no idea what kind of anger the other spouse still harbors. So if we're the spouse mired in the anger we can't overcome, who is the only person we're hurting? Ourselves! In order for us to move on, we *must* learn how to forgive and forget.

I must admit that forgetting is harder for me than forgiving. I have the memory of an elephant and that's not always a good thing! I can tell you what I wore to a movie five years ago or what I gave you for Christmas the last ten years in a row. So while I work very hard at forgiving people, it sometimes takes me longer to forget. But forget I must—because then and only then can I set myself free.

Finally, a huge part of forgiveness is that I must forgive myself. I'll say that again: *I must forgive myself.* I have often thought that if I treated my friends as shabbily as I treat myself, I wouldn't have any friends. I am my own worst enemy. Why am I so hard on myself? Well, being a perfectionist doesn't help matters any! That is why I work so hard on this particular character flaw—I know I will never be able to meet my own standards if I think I always have to be perfect.

So I try very hard to cut myself a little slack. I need to understand that the first person I need to forgive is myself. I'm coming to realize that my life is a work in progress—I'm doing the best I can and that's good enough! Sure, I'll make mistakes or errors in judgment—we all do. But when I do, I need to deal with the situation at hand and then move on. It is not easy for me and I don't think it ever will be. But I constantly work on it and I'm slowly making progress. Because I know it's the only way I can set myself free—free to live my life the best I can every single day.

# *Powerlessness*

*All our natural powers can be used mightily by God, but only when we think nothing of them, and surrender ourselves to be simply the vehicles of divine power, letting God use us as He wills, content to be even despised by men if He be glorified.*

—*G.H. Knight*

The terms "powerless" and "helpless" are not always synonymous and in the context discussed here, it's important to understand that. Step 1 of all 12-step programs says we must admit we're powerless over our addiction. Step 2 says we must turn our lives over to the care of the Higher Power of our choice and allow him/her/it to do for us what we cannot do for ourselves. The 12 steps are in a particular order for a reason. You can't go on to the remaining ten steps until you've worked Steps 1 and 2.

To admit that we are powerless to change our lives and realize that we must turn them over to our Higher Power requires great courage and faith. We are allowing someone else to be in charge of our life. We are no longer in control! When we take this great leap of faith, we are consciously choosing to become powerless—this is an active and assertive decision.

Being powerless in this sense is the exact opposite of being helpless. If we are helpless, we are acting very passively—we have in essence given up. But when we admit our powerlessness, we are acting very positively—we are choosing to turn our life over to our Higher Power.

And here is the best part: when we honestly and completely turn our lives over to our Higher Power, we set ourselves free! Isn't that wonderful? That giant cinderblock that was permanently affixed to our shoulders disappears. We are now able to pursue our life, one day at a time, secure in the knowledge that someone else is in charge. And *that* someone has a plan for our lives that is beyond our wildest imagination. All we have to do is show up every day, ready and willing to live our lives to the fullest.

# Prayer and Meditation

*Be still, and know that I am God...*

*—Psalm 46:10, NIV*

*Half an hour's meditation is essential except when you're very busy. Then a full hour is needed.*

*—Saint Francis of Sales*

Prayer and meditation go hand in hand. Prayer is when I talk to God; meditation is when God talks to me. I have found that it is critical to my mental and emotional health to set aside time every day to pray and meditate. And like one of the quotes above says, the busier I am, the more I need this quiet time with myself and with God.

Having some quiet time each day keeps me centered and focused. What do I do during my quiet time? I read several meditations. I talk to God about what's going on in my life and what I need His help with. I close my eyes and quietly wait for God to speak to me.

When do I do this? I try to create my quiet time when I get up each morning and again before I go to bed at night. For me, starting and ending the day with prayer and meditation keep me on track. But it doesn't really matter *when* you pray and meditate—what's important is that you make it part of your daily life.

Where you spend your quiet time, however, *is* important. It needs to be somewhere you can be by yourself—a haven set aside for you and you alone. You might find it soothing to play some soft background music or perhaps light some candles—whatever it takes to create an environment of peace and serenity.

In the past few years, I have come to realize that I am an unwilling participant in this age of advanced technology. Oh, I have all the "toys" I need to function in this crazy world—computer, e-mail, cell phone, digital camera—the list is almost endless. And I have made myself keep up to date with all the latest technology because I refuse to let the world pass me by. But I fight it kicking and screaming every day—I hate it!

It drives me crazy to:

- be in an airport and realize everyone is talking on a cell phone but me

- walk by someone's office and see them talking on their desk phone, waiting to answer their ringing cell phone, and checking their Blackberry for any messages they have received in the last 20 seconds

- open my personal e-mail at home and see 23 unread messages that weren't there yesterday and *all* of them are spam

I miss and long for:

- a visit from a friend

- a handwritten note

- lunch in a restaurant uninterrupted by people talking on their cell phones

- quiet time—away from computers, TVs, cell phones and all the rest

It's no wonder most of us often question our sanity—in this age of information overload, there's no way we can retain all we see, hear, and read. And I for one have a problem getting rid of the garbage meandering aimlessly through my brain and keeping what's important!

Because of the fast-paced world we live in, it is even more critical for us to carve out some time every day for prayer and meditation.

# *Timing*

*If you want to see God laugh, plan your life!*

*—Anon.*

*A coincidence may be God's way of acting anonymously in your life.*

*—Anon.*

There have been countless times in my life when I was sure I knew exactly what I needed and when I needed it. Imagine my great disappointment when events didn't unfold according to my plan and my timetable! When I don't get what I think I need, I rant and rave at God, asking Him why I can't have whatever it is I need so badly and why I can't have it right now. When I'm sad or depressed, I cry out to God, asking Him why I have to suffer like this. Haven't I suffered enough for one lifetime? Can't He spread the sadness around for a change instead of dumping it all on me?

When my "pity party" is over and some semblance of sanity returns, I know that God didn't dump this sadness on me. Rather, I believe that God is sad when I'm sad, He weeps when I weep, and He rejoices when I rejoice.

Do I question God's timing? Constantly! I have wondered many times why it took so long for me to come out of the fog and start to really live. And I'm forever wishing I could have figured all this out ten years earlier than I did. But my therapist gently reminds me that I might not have survived if I had come out of the fog any sooner. And I'm coming to realize that there's no way I can recapture any of the years I've already lived.

And then I begin to ask myself: What if everything that has happened in my life happened for a reason exactly when it was supposed to? What if I needed all that time to learn the lessons I needed to learn? What if I'm exactly where I need to be right now? The day I start to believe this is the day I can humbly and willingly turn my life over to God—I can truly "let go and let God."

In my heart of hearts, I believe I am a unique child of God and that He loves me unconditionally. I believe He has a plan for me that contains treasures beyond my wildest imagination. I don't have to have all the answers or know what that plan or timetable is—I'm only human and that's not my job. My job is to believe in His plan for me and be a willing participant as I watch it unfold, day by marvelous day.

# Feeling *all* our feelings...

# Feelings

*We are neither weak nor deficient for indulging in our feelings. It means we're becoming healthy and whole.*

*—Melody Beattie, <u>Beyond Codependency</u>*

*Some of my feelings have been stored so long they have freezer burn.*

*—Ibid.*

I'm involved with the Stephen Ministry program at my church and I teach various classes to our trainees. One of my favorite classes is "Feelings: Yours, Mine and Ours."

When I was preparing my lesson plan the first time, I couldn't imagine filling a two-hour class discussing feelings. Now that I've taught the class several times, I have found that two hours isn't nearly long enough!

I believe we often deal with feelings in one of two ways: we either give them too much importance or we ignore them. Neither one works!

Feelings are feelings—it's that simple. They aren't "good" or "bad"—they just *are*. The most important thing to realize is that the only way to deal with our feelings is to acknowledge them, accept them, work through them, and then let them go.

Any time we ignore our feelings, we are just delaying the business of dealing with them. They aren't going anywhere. Sooner or later they will re-appear—sometimes when we least expect them and often at a most inappropriate time.

In the household I grew up in, we often didn't deal with our feelings. We were more interested in what others thought about us than who we really were and what we were feeling. We swept many of our problems under the rug so we wouldn't have to discuss them. Looking back, it's not surprising to me that I ended up in a marriage where we didn't discuss our feelings either. Both of us became very clever at creating a façade for others to see and judge us by. And we

47

succeeded, so that it became harder and harder for me to differentiate between the real me and the persona I had created for others to see.

Naturally, when I finally came out of my fog, I was overwhelmed by all the feelings that engulfed me. At first, most of them were sad ones. As time went by, some happy feelings began to trickle in, until eventually I realized I was experiencing all kinds of feelings.

Sometimes when I'm having a difficult time trying to work through my feelings, I wonder if I wouldn't be better off if I didn't have any at all. That way, I wouldn't be sad when I lose someone I love or disappointed when I don't get that promotion I'm so sure I deserve. But then I realize that I also would never experience the happiness of finding a new friend or be moved to tears when I see a beautiful sunset over the ocean.

We are made to be human and to experience all of our feelings. And God will be there with us through all of them. That's His promise to us.

In the pages that follow, I will discuss some of our most common feelings in more detail, including anger, depression, grief, happiness, hope, humiliation, loneliness, and love.

# ANGER

*If you are never angry, then you are unborn.*

*—African Proverb*

*Holding on to anger is like grasping a hot coal with the intent of throwing it at someone else; you are the one getting burned.*

*—Buddha*

It's o.k. to get angry. Really—it's o.k.! For years I didn't think "nice" people got mad. I stuffed my anger and swept it under the rug, but the funny thing is that it kept popping out at the most inopportune times. That's the thing about anger—if we don't acknowledge it, it will jump up and bite us when we least expect it.

Too many Christians think they shouldn't get angry, so they stuff that feeling until it erupts. But think about it—wasn't Jesus angry when he chased the money changers out of the temple? So He'll surely understand if we get mad, even at Him. I have yelled and screamed at Him many times, asking Him why He's letting this thing or that happen to me, and you know what? He's still there for me and He still loves me. He was made human to walk on this earth in our shoes and to feel our feelings. That's why it's o.k. for us to get angry—He understands.

I have found that one of the best ways to deal with my anger is to write about it. Sometimes I use my computer and sometimes I write in longhand—once I was so mad that I ripped the sheets of paper I was writing on! But the wonderful thing is that writing acts as a catharsis—it clears my mind and I always feel better afterwards. After writing about my anger, I have sometimes been able to have a civil conversation with the person who made me mad and explain why his or her actions are not acceptable to me.

There's one more part to this piece—we need to ask ourselves if we have contributed to the situation. That's hard because it means we must recognize and accept responsibility for our behavior. Sometimes we have contributed and sometimes we haven't. The best way for me to figure this out is to remove myself from the situation and take some time to think. When I can look at things more objectively and honestly, then and only then can I decide whether or not I'm at fault, either partially or totally. If I am, I apologize and move on.

Remember, anger is just a feeling. It's not a good feeling or a bad feeling—it's just a feeling. And, like all feelings, it must be dealt with—preferably when it occurs. Then and only then can we accept it, deal with it, let it go, and move on.

# DEPRESSION

*There is no vulture like despair.*

—*Voltaire*

*The worst sorrows in life are not its losses and misfortunes, but its fears.*

—*A. C. Snow*

"Depression" and "depressed" are both words that are overused these days. We often say, "I'm so depressed." But we probably aren't talking about being clinically depressed—more often than not, we're experiencing some form of temporary sadness or misfortune. That doesn't make what we're going through any less painful—it just means we'll be able to work through it fairly quickly and start to feel better on our own.

Clinical depression, on the other hand, is a serious physical problem which usually requires professional help and/or medication. Note that I said clinical depression is a "serious *physical* problem." If you are clinically depressed, you have a chemical imbalance in your brain that is best treated with antidepressant medication.

One of the problems about depression is that we often don't know that we're depressed. I know now that I was probably depressed for many years before I realized it. I just plodded along, day after miserable day, thinking that was how it was supposed to be. WRONG! After being in therapy and on antidepressants for several years now, I know I don't have to lead a miserable life. There are some steps I can take to help myself—the choice is up to me.

I almost choked on the first antidepressant pill I took. I felt like I was "wimping out"—why couldn't I just suck it up and take care of this all by myself? But then I remembered what my physician had said: "If you broke your leg, would you think twice about getting it set?" Of course not. Then why did I have such a problem taking medication that could help control another physical illness, a chemical imbalance in my brain? Thankfully, I was finally able to come to terms with this.

What is so sad is that there is still a stigma attached to depression and mental illness. When I was a teenager, I remember reading a half-page ad that an older businessman had placed in our local newspaper. The gist of his message was that he had been hospitalized for depression but he wanted to assure his customers that he was much better now and that he was back at work fulltime. When I read that ad many years ago, I was shocked that this man would "air his dirty laundry" for the whole town to see. As I think about it now, I am struck by how much courage it took for him to admit he was depressed, especially using such a public forum.

Having been closely associated with several people who have been clinically depressed, I know what a debilitating illness it is. Unlike recovering from a broken leg, there is no timetable for healing when you're dealing with depression. In fact, it is an illness that is more often brought under control than cured. The other difficulty is that there is no one magic antidepressant medication for everyone. We often have to try several different ones (or a combination of them) before we find out what works for us. This sometimes takes a while, and getting our medication regulated can become yet another frustration for us during this time.

All of the books on depression I have ever read include a check list similar to the one below as a guide to determine if you or someone you know is suffering from clinical depression. If *five* or more of the symptoms listed below last for *more than two weeks*, please consult a doctor as soon as possible. There is help out there—you do not have to suffer alone. In many cases, clinical depression can be successfully treated with medication and therapy.

Here are the symptoms:

- Feelings of sadness or irritability

- Loss of interest or pleasure in activities once enjoyed

- Changes in weight or appetite

- Feeling guilty, hopeless or worthless

- Inability to concentrate, remember things or make decisions

- Fatigue or loss of energy

- Restlessness or decreased activity noticed by others

- Complaints of physical aches and pains for which no medical cause can be found

- Thoughts of suicide or death

# GRIEF

*Your grief will take more energy than you would have ever imagined.*

*—Therese Rando*

*An ungrieved loss remains forever alive in our unconscious, which has no sense of time.*

*—Charles L. Whitfield*

More than once I have heard someone ask, "How long does grief last?" There's only one answer: "As long as it takes." How we work through our grief is as unique as our fingerprints. There is no timetable for grief, and it does us no good to compare ourselves to others. Eliminate thoughts like "I *should* be over this by now!" from your mind. As long as you're trying to work through your grief, even if it feels like you're taking one step forward and two steps backward, that's all that matters.

Over the course of a lifetime, we will be exposed to many kinds of grief, including losing a loved one, losing a job or not getting a promotion, going through a separation and divorce, losing a beloved pet, or declaring bankruptcy. In fact, I'm going to go out on a limb and say there's not one of us who hasn't experienced some form of grief in our lives—and the chances are good that we'll experience more grief before we die. If you have never grieved, you are most likely in extreme denial and are completely out of touch with reality.

Although each of us grieves in our own way, there are certain similarities in all grieving processes. These "stages of grief" were first defined by Elisabeth Kübler-Ross in her groundbreaking book, *On Death and Dying*. They are denial, anger, bargaining, depression, and—finally—acceptance.

All of us must go through all these stages as we work through our grief, and work through it we must unless we want to remain stuck in one of the stages. And let me caution you—these five stages of grief aren't tied up in a neat little package with a pretty ribbon on top. For example, you won't experience denial for a while, then move straight to anger, and on through stages three, four, and five. I wish it were that easy! In most cases, you will go through denial first and arrive at some type of acceptance last, but beyond that you'll probably move all over the place. These stages don't necessarily come in order, and once you've gone through a particular stage doesn't mean it won't pop up again.

In the last few years, I have lost several friends and close family members (including my mother). Most recently, I went through the pain of having to have my beloved golden retriever put to sleep. Because I have experienced "up close and personal" grief, I want to share a few thoughts with you that may help ease your pain someday.

- Grieving is hard work. I want to say that again: *Grieving is hard work.* It is emotionally draining and you'll experience a tiredness that doesn't go away with a good night's sleep. My mother died very suddenly and after I got over the initial shock, I spent a lot of time sitting on my sofa staring at the walls. I was rendered totally immobile by my grief.

- It's o.k. to cry. Really. In fact, it's practically essential to the grieving process. It's one of the first steps we take when we grieve any loss.

- It's o.k. to be angry. Really. I have already discussed anger and the fact that it's just another feeling we have to deal with or it will smack us in the face at the most inopportune time. So let your anger out—at the loved one who died or asked for a divorce, at the boss for firing you, at God for letting this happen to you. Two good ways to express your anger are screaming while you're driving down the road (make sure your windows are closed!) and beating a tennis racket on the bed while at the same time screaming why you're angry. Be solicitous of others when you express your anger, but do it!

- Take as long as you need to grieve, within reason. If you're still in the denial stage five years after the event you're grieving happened, you'll need to explore what's wrong. But don't let anyone tell you how long you should grieve or that you should be farther along than you are. There is no timetable involved with grief. Only you will know how long it takes.

- Join a grief support group. This is so important! You can't imagine how healing it is to be with others who are grieving too—it "normalizes" your grief a bit and lets you know others understand much of what you're going through—they have been there too. Often, after a short period of time, you'll find that family and friends have moved on to other things in their lives and they may not be interested in hearing you talk about your grief any longer. That's why a support group is so helpful. You can share your feelings (or just listen if you prefer) and know that others will understand and sympathize with you.

- Know that things will get better. Sometimes when we're in a deep hole that we can't begin to crawl out of, we wonder if life will ever be worth living again. Trust me—it will! If we work through our grief, over time we'll come to realize that there are some bright spots in our days. There may be more sadness than joy in the beginning, but the day will come when the joy outweighs the sadness. It's so important to believe that no matter how sad you feel, there will be a time when you'll feel better.

- Finally—and most important—take care of yourself as you grieve. Most of us forget to do that and we suffer, both physically and emotionally. Realize that everything will take longer—this includes getting up in the morning (sometimes you won't feel like doing even that), getting dressed, going to work, going to church, etc. It's as if you're moving through the days in slow motion. Get some physical exercise each day, eat healthily, try to get a good night's sleep, and set aside a certain time each day to meditate and pray.

In the end, we'll be a stronger person for having worked through our grief. And we'll be more compassionate with others when they go down a similar path, as they surely will.

# HAPPINESS

*The happiness of life is made up of minute fractions—the little soon-forgotten charities of a kiss or smile, a kind look, a heartfelt compliment, and the countless infinitestimals of pleasurable and genial feeling.*

—*William Taylor Coleridge*

*Happiness is not a state to arrive at but a manner of traveling.*

—*Margaret Lee Runbeck*

In one of the first 12-step meetings I attended, I heard someone say, "Life is a journey, not a destination." I was totally blown away! That simple but profound statement has changed my life. You see, I always thought happiness was something that was just beyond my reach even though I was constantly seeking it. In my mind, happiness was like the pot of gold at the end of the rainbow—I kept hoping if I worked really hard all my life, maybe I would find happiness before I died.

It took me a while to believe in my heart that life is indeed a journey but when I did, something magical happened: I was actually able to find pockets of happiness many times each day! It is here and now, just waiting for us to enjoy and cherish—a bright red cardinal sitting on a bare tree branch in the dead of winter; the infectious laughter of a small child the first time he sees his new puppy; the joy of listening to an orchestra perform a beautiful piece of music—and the list goes on and on.

Sometimes I feel sad when I think of all the moments of happiness I've missed in my life. But at the same time, I'm very thankful that I've discovered what happiness is all about so I won't miss out on another single minute of it.

Maybe I'm finally looking at the glass half full!

# HOPE

*He who has a why for life can put up with any how.*

*—Frederick Nietzsche*

*There is nothing in the world, I venture to say, that would so effectively help one to survive even the worst conditions as the knowledge that there is a meaning in one's life.*

*—Viktor Frankl*

Several years ago, a very kind relative of mine graciously offered to spend a Saturday with me so we could discuss what was happening in my life and possibly discover what effect my childhood years had in making me the person I now was. My relative was also a physician and a friend, so he was able to discuss this life of mine on several different levels. I shall be forever grateful to him for his counsel and his time.

He asked me to read *Man's Search for Meaning* by Viktor Frankl before our meeting. He said he often suggested that his patients read this book and he thought it would be of help to me too.

I read the book and discovered that Frankl was a renowned psychotherapist and a Holocaust survivor. Many of his family members (including his wife and parents) died in concentration camps. He wrote *Man's Search for Meaning* to describe his experiences in four Nazi death camps, including Auschwitz. He came to believe that man's primary reason for living is the search for meaning, and he later helped his patients find the personal meaning in their lives, no matter how dismal they might be.

He chose to write about his experiences in Nazi concentration camps because he hoped if others knew he could survive such a terrible ordeal they might come to believe they could find meaning in their lives as well.

This is a wonderful book. It is a book about hope—no matter how lonely or depressed or sad we might be, as long as we have hope we can make it. People who commit suicide have lost all hope. They are probably lonely and depressed and sad too, but it's when they lose hope that they lose the will to live. This is so sad because the solution to their problem might be just around the corner but they don't live to see it. Suicide is a permanent solution to what is often a temporary problem.

When we're in the depths of despair, what are some things that could give us hope? Those things would surely vary among individuals. But coming from one who has been there, here are a couple of things that helped me:

- Knowing it's temporary. As compared to my years of living in a fog when my world was gray and bleak day after day with no hope for improvement, I now know that things *will* get better. The hole I'm in may be just as deep as it ever was, but the time it takes me to crawl out of it and re-enter the real world will be much shorter. So if I'm having a really bad day, it helps me immensely to be able to say to myself—and believe—that I'll feel better tomorrow or the next day. And in the meantime, I remind myself it's o.k. if I go into what I call my "survival mode"—doing just the basics to get by and being kind to myself until I'm feeling better.

- Having faith—hope is closely tied to faith. I know now that God doesn't desert me, nor does he shower me with bad stuff willy-nilly. My faith helps me through rough times because, again, I know those times are temporary.

I remind myself over and over again that we're all going to have some bad times in our lives—there's nothing we can do about that. When they do come along, we need to figure out how to deal with them in a healthy way. Hope is one of the best tools we have to get through the bad—and the good—times in our lives.

# HUMILIATION

*In certain moments a single almost insignificant sorrow may, by association, bring together all the little relics of pain and discomfort, bodily or mental, that we have endured even from infancy.*

—*Samuel Taylor Coleridge*

I have lived with the fear of humiliation all my life, and I am just now coming to realize what an impact that fear has had on me.

A particularly vivid example comes to mind. One drizzly day when I was in the eighth grade, my mother *made* me wear a raincoat and rubber boots to school. I was mortified and tried to talk her out of it, but she insisted. Guess what happened? By the time I got off the bus at school, the sun was shining brightly! Of course I felt like a complete idiot—I wanted to crawl under the bus until the bell rang.

Imagine my total humiliation when a couple of people in the "in crowd" (something I was definitely not part of!) made fun of me and my rain gear in front of several of their friends. I still remember the names of the people who made fun of me and what they said after all these years; and while I'm sure they have long since forgotten this incident, I never have. To this day, I can never decide whether or not to wear a raincoat or take an umbrella. When I do, it doesn't rain; when I don't, it does!

Isn't it amazing how we, as adults, can be so deeply affected by incidents which happened in our formative years? For me, the six years of junior and senior high school were particularly traumatic. I was trying so hard to fit in that I became a "people pleaser" extraordinaire. But, alas, I never fit in. In fact, it seemed that the harder I tried to fit in, the more I stood out. In today's lingo, I would have been called a "nerd"—I was a smart, overweight introvert with low self-esteem, and I lacked all but the most basic social skills. No wonder I was always a wallflower when I went to parties. In my mind, at least (and perception is *everything* when you're a teenager), I stood out like a sore thumb wherever I was and whatever I was doing—when all I ever wanted to do was fade into the wood-work and be "just like everyone else."

Fast forward to the present day. How does the fear of humiliation still impact my life—years and years after the incident in junior high school? In countless ways, both big and small. I'm scared to ask anyone in the grocery store where an item is. In fact, I have left a store without buying something I couldn't find more times that I can remember. I am terrified of doing something by myself for the first time. That includes everything from pumping my own gas (a huge challenge and ultimate victory for me), to going to church alone, to going to social gatherings and meeting new people.

I have asked myself many times why these things bother me so much. I have finally figured out it's because I'm very concerned about what other people think of me—way too concerned. I was scared to pump my own gas because I didn't know how and I was afraid other people at the gas station would laugh at me and think I was stupid. I was afraid everyone at church would feel sorry for me because I was there alone.

What am I doing to myself? Two things, it seems to me. First, I'm giving way too much credence to other people and what they may or may not be thinking. Most people probably have more important things to do than sit around laughing at someone who's having trouble pumping gas.

Second, I am depriving myself of many wonderful experiences on this journey that is my life. The choice is mine. I can sit home day after day surfing the Web and operating the remote control on my TV, or I can take a risk once in a while and step outside my comfort zone to try a new adventure. And you know what? The first time is by far the hardest. The second time is easier, the third time is easier still, and pretty soon it's a snap! Things which seemed impossible not long ago are now a breeze.

Does it take courage? You bet! Do I feel good when I do it? Absolutely! I find myself on a natural "high" that is indescribable.

What a valuable lesson to learn. You see, I am my own worst enemy, and I know now that my fear of humiliation began to take root all those years ago when a vulnerable eighth grader was ridiculed in front of her peers. Maybe someday I'll be able to let go of her—and of her fear.

# LONELINESS

*To live one's life in a body that one cannot feel is, I believe, the loneliest lone-liness.*

—*James J. Lynch*

Did you know you can be lonely without being alone? It's true. Some of the loneliest times I ever spent were when I was with other people. I didn't realize it at the time—I always associated loneliness with being alone. How could I be lonely when I was around other people?

And did you know you don't have to be lonely when you're alone? I never knew that. When my marriage was breaking up, one of my greatest fears was that since I would be alone, I would also be lonely. Somehow, having another living, breathing human being in the house was better than the alternative.

How can you be alone without being lonely? I must say that when I first moved into my own place, I was both alone and lonely. But I know now that I craved and needed that time of serenity in my life. After living for years flitting from one crisis to the next, the absence of stress in my life was truly a blessing. That peaceful interlude gave me time to reflect—to read and meditate and pray. It gave me time to come to grips with who I was and what I wanted to do "when I grew up"! It gave me the opportunity to think about starting my life over—as an individual, not as half of a couple.

It wasn't easy. Sometimes I wished I had kids so I could throw myself into their lives and not deal with mine. But that was not God's plan for me. I had to come face to face with myself and it was scary. But it was also the period of my greatest growth and enlightenment. My mind, body, and soul were refreshed and restored, and I knew then it was time for me to be about getting on with my life, including figuring out how not to be lonely.

So how does one go about the business of not being lonely? One thing for sure—it won't happen as long as you sit home in your recliner hitting your remote control button. I know—I tried that! About the only thing that felt better was my index finger because it was getting so much exercise!

Solving the loneliness riddle involves reaching out to others. It involves taking risks and allowing yourself to become vulnerable. For introverts like me, this is particularly difficult. It was so much easier to sit home and feel sorry for myself.

How did I do it specifically? I made myself get out of the recliner and start going to 12-step meetings; I joined a divorce support group; I started seeing a therapist; I started to become more active in my church by joining a circle and a

Sunday School class. For me, being active in the church doesn't mean sitting in the sanctuary for an hour every Sunday!

By forcing myself to participate in these various activities, I slowly began to make some friends. In my 12-step meetings and divorce support group, I drew on the strengths of others in similar circumstances to help me through the tough times. Slowly, I began to transition back into the real world. I wish I could tell you it went smoothly but that would be a lie. There were times when I could reach out to others and participate in various activities but there were also times when I needed to fall back and regroup and be by myself. But even when I did that, I began to realize that I wasn't as lonely in my solitude as I had been before.

By far the most important work I did was on myself. Because I had such low self-esteem, I knew this would be hard. I came to understand that our best friend and our worst enemy both reside within us. It's our choice which person we choose to be. I learned that self-love isn't selfish, it's critical to my survival. I learned it's o.k. to take care of myself because no one else will. And I learned that God has always loved me and He's always there with me—if there is a distance between us, it's because I created the gap because He hasn't moved.

Mostly I learned that I am o.k. just the way I am right now. I am a child of God and I am loved. I can celebrate who I am by honoring where I came from and anticipating where I'm going. But right this very minute, I can love myself and be content with my life. It's a wonderful feeling!

# LOVE

*Someone has written that love makes people believe in immortality, because there seems not to be room enough in life for so great a tenderness.*

—*Robert Louis Stevenson*

*The most important thing in life is to learn how to give out love, and to let it come in.*

—*Morrie Schwartz*

Love is the greatest and most wondrous feeling of all. It surrounds us with a sense of joy, peace, and contentment—in fact, it permeates our very being. Words can't adequately describe what love is, although poets and writers have tried to capture its essence since the beginning of recorded time.

Love is a wonderful paradox—the more we give away, the more we get in return. It's like a snowball—love just grows and grows and grows!

There are many kinds of love—love of our fellow man, love of that special someone in our life, love of family and friends, and even puppy love. But by far the most important kinds of love we need in our lives are love of God and love of self. Indeed, until we come to love ourselves and realize that we are lovable, we aren't capable of giving and receiving love.

Many of us who grew up in dysfunctional households may not have received the unconditional love we needed while we were growing up. Sadly, we might not even realize this until later in our lives, if ever. It's very possible that our parents or other family members simply weren't capable of giving us love. Or perhaps they couldn't verbalize their love (by saying, "I love you.") or demonstrate their love (with a hug, a caress, or a smile). Or maybe their love was conditional and had strings attached—perhaps we had to jump through certain hoops before we could receive that love. It may take us a while but hopefully we'll eventually come to understand that whatever the reasons, it's not our fault we didn't get the love we needed.

If we were deprived of unconditional love in those important growing-up years, we'll probably pay the consequences later on. We may not trust anyone. Or we may be so starved for love and affection that we become promiscuous. Or we may build a wall around ourselves and refuse to let anyone get close because we're terrified of intimacy—we may be distant or even frigid for the same reason. We may play games and give our love conditionally because that's the only kind of love we know.

In order to experience love completely, we must tear down that wall and allow ourselves to become vulnerable. We must be willing to share our innermost feelings with someone else. This can be very scary because if we allow ourselves to become vulnerable, we also risk the possibility of being hurt. If we feel like we've already been hurt enough in our lifetime, it may be hard for us to reach out in love again.

That would be very sad because we would miss out on so much. The place to start is with ourselves. We must reach deep into our souls and tell ourselves over and over again that we are good enough just the way we are and that God loves us. What's important is for us to come to love ourselves. We must work diligently to erase those negative tapes that keep running through our heads telling us we aren't good enough. Yes we are!

Our mantra should be, "I am good enough. I am a loving person. God loves me." We must keep repeating this mantra until we believe it with all our heart—then and only then can we replace those old, negative tapes.

Imagine a world filled with love, not hate; with harmony, not chaos; with peace, not war; with humility, not stubborn pride; with kindness, not anger. I believe we can live in a world like this and I believe it is up to each one of us to do our part to make that happen.

Opening ourselves up to love is a joyous, freeing experience. When we truly come to love ourselves, we can begin to reach out to others in love. We come to realize that our lives would be empty indeed if we closed everyone out just to avoid being hurt. And take my word for it—we will be simply amazed at the love that is out there waiting for us. All we have to do is have the great courage to reach out for it.

# Moving toward wholeness—slowly, surely…

# *Beauty*

*Though we travel the world over to find the beautiful, we must carry it with us or we find it not.*

—*Ralph Waldo Emerson*

*Beauty is altogether in the eye of the beholder.*

—*General Lew Wallace*

Some of the most beautiful people I have ever known were not classic beauties. By that I mean they wouldn't have won any beauty contests and you would never have seen them modeling the latest fashions on a Paris runway. Why is that? Because their beauty came from within and it made them absolutely radiant.

I'm thinking of a particular woman I know. She is just "average" looking on the outside—you wouldn't give her a second glance if you passed her on the street. But oh, how her beauty shines from within! The minute you start talking to her, she captivates you, and you are aware of the love and genuine interest she has in you. As long as she's talking to you, you have her undivided attention—you are the only person in her life. I have truly never known a more beautiful person.

What a shame it is that many of us judge ourselves and our beauty by the people we see on TV and in the movies. And I have a real bone to pick with advertisers who bombard us with ads almost always containing young, thin (even emaciated) actors. No wonder so many of us have low self-esteem! If these are the people we choose as our role models, we are in deep trouble. It is rare indeed that an ad depicts what I call "real life" or "real people." And it's very important to realize that what we're seeing on TV or in the movies is *not* real life or real people.

Eleanor Roosevelt and Mother Teresa were not particularly attractive physically—but the way they lived their lives radiated an inner beauty that could never be extinguished. Remember this: true beauty *always* comes from within. It comes from our hearts and our souls as we go about being kind and loving and giving and gentle and caring. And inward beauty can't be altered by age or disease—it never leaves us.

Someone e-mailed me the following story and I must share it with you because it's a lovely description of the meaning of true beauty:

## Ugly The Tomcat

Everyone in the apartment complex I lived in knew who Ugly was. Ugly was the resident tomcat. Ugly loved three things in this world: fighting, eating garbage, and, shall we say, love.

The combination of these things combined with a life spent outside had their effect on Ugly. To start with, he had only one eye and where the other should have been was a hole. He was also missing his ear on the same side, his left foot appeared to have been badly broken at one time, and had healed at an unnatural angle, making him look like he was always turning the corner.

Ugly would have been a dark gray tabby, striped type, except for the sores covering his head, neck, and even his shoulders.

Every time someone saw Ugly there was the same reaction. "That's one UGLY cat!!!"

All the children were warned not to touch him, the adults threw rocks at him, hosed him down, squirted him when he tried to come in their homes, or shut his paws in the door when he would not leave. Ugly always had the same reaction.

If you turned the hose on him, he would stand there, getting soaked until you gave up and quit. If you threw things at him, he would curl his lanky body around your feet in forgiveness.

Whenever he spied children, he would come running, meowing frantically and bump his head against their hands, begging for their love.

If you ever picked him up he would immediately begin suckling on your shirt, earrings, whatever he could find.

One day Ugly shared his love with the neighbor's dogs. They did not respond kindly, and Ugly was badly mauled. I tried to rush to his aid. By the time I got to where he was laying, it was apparent Ugly's sad life was almost at an end.

As I picked him up and tried to carry him home, I could hear him wheezing and gasping, and could feel him struggling. It must be hurting him terribly, I thought.

Then I felt a familiar tugging, sucking sensation on my ear. Ugly, in so much pain, suffering and obviously dying, was trying to suckle my ear. I pulled him closer to me, and he bumped the palm of my hand with his head, then he turned his one golden eye towards me, and I could hear the distinct sound of purring.

Even in the greatest pain, that ugly battled scarred cat was asking for only a little affection, perhaps some compassion.

At that moment I thought Ugly was the most beautiful, loving creature I had ever seen. Never once did he try to bite or scratch me, try to get away from me, or struggle in any way. Ugly just looked up at me completely trusting in me to relieve his pain.

Ugly died in my arms before I could get inside, but I sat and held him for a long time afterwards, thinking about how one scarred, deformed little stray could so alter my opinion about what it means to have true pureness of spirit, to love so totally and truly.

Ugly taught me more about giving and compassion than a thousand books, lectures, or talk show specials ever could, and for that I will always be thankful. He had been scarred on the outside, but I was scarred on the inside, and it was time for me to move on and learn to love truly and deeply. To give my total to those I cared for.

*Many people want to be richer, more successful,*
*well liked, beautiful, but for me…*

*I will always try to be Ugly.*

—Author Unknown

# Change

*Life belongs to the living, and he who lives must be prepared for changes.*

*—Goethe*

*One cannot step twice into the same river, for the water into which you first stepped has flowed on.*

*—Herakleitos*

I don't like change. I'm a creature of habit, I guess, because I subscribe to the theory that "if it ain't broke, don't fix it"! But over the years, I've begun to ask myself why I'm so afraid of change. Some of the answers I came up with are pretty revealing.

Trying to function in a world where addictions were prevalent, I constantly yearned for anything that was steady and concrete. So much of my life was out of control that I clung to anything that was familiar. I craved the routine monotony of my life because it made me feel safe and secure. I was terrified of change because it was yet another thing I couldn't control.

I have learned that fear of change is fear of the unknown, and most of us are afraid of, or at least apprehensive about, the unknown. We're perfectly content to remain in our "comfort zone" and not venture into uncharted waters. What a shame that is! Think of everything we miss by limiting our experiences to those that are familiar to us. The unknown doesn't have to be scary if we think of it as a grand adventure and an exciting challenge.

The most important thing I have learned is that change is inevitable—as inevitable as breathing—and it happens almost as frequently! So as long as we are on this planet, we're going to experience change. Whether we embrace it or fight it kicking and screaming all our lives is up to us.

The saddest part about change is that most of us don't embrace it. We plod through life griping about this and that and getting mired down in minutiae. You see, it takes courage to move out of our comfort zone and test our fledgling wings. But once we do, we realize how wonderful and freeing it is, and we know we can never go back.

# *Comparisons*

*To envy another's situation is only a way that we compare our insides to other's outsides.*

—*Stephanie Ericsson*

When my father was suffering through many years of debilitating illness, my mother once said to me: "Look at those people driving down the street. I wish I could trade places with them!" I know what she meant. Her life was so miserable right then—surely the people in that car were better off and happier than she was.

It's an easy trap to fall into. I do it all the time. When I'm having a particularly difficult day emotionally, I look at the people all around me at work or at church and wonder how they can be so happy when I'm so sad. I don't have a husband or any children and sometimes it seems to me that everyone *but* me is married and has children (or some combination thereof). And of course I have visions that they're the perfect family—you know, like the ones we see on a greeting card: mother, father, children, dog, and the proverbial picket fence. That's when it's very easy for me to think, "Poor me—everyone is happy but me. Woe is me."

But are they really happy? They certainly could be, but they could just as easily be miserable. Looking at someone driving down the street won't tell me anything about what's going on in their lives because appearances can definitely be deceiving!

The one thing I do know is this: the only person responsible for my happiness is me. The minute I start expecting other people or things to make me happy is when I move from reality into fantasy. I could be laid off from the job that makes me happy. That perfect love relationship could end tomorrow. The money I win in the lottery can easily be spent.

So if I'm counting on my job or my significant other or lots of money or—you fill in the blank—to make me happy, I'm probably in for a big disappointment somewhere down the road.

The relationships I need to honor and nurture are those with myself and with God. And when I do this, I will stay centered and, miraculously, everything will fall into place according to His will and His timing.

# Courage

*You must do the things you think you cannot do.*

*—Eleanor Roosevelt*

*Courage is the greatest of all virtues, because if you haven't courage, you may not have an opportunity to use any of the others.*

*—Samuel Johnson*

A special friend once told me that he was in awe of me because I had more courage than anyone he knew. I was amazed to hear him say that and, as is often my wont, I "pooh-poohed" his honest words of praise, belittling both him and me in the process.

"Me, courageous?" I thought to myself. "All I'm doing is trying to survive. What's so courageous about that?"

Until a few years ago, I equated courage with being "macho"—you know, he-men like Sylvester Stallone and Arnold Schwarzenegger and the roles they played. Well, Rocky and the Terminator may or may not be courageous characters, but the words "macho" and "courageous" are not synonymous.

How do I define courage? For me, courage means facing my fear and doing it anyway. I spent a lot of years being anything *but* courageous—if I was afraid to do something or if it was too hard, I just didn't do it or I let someone else do it for me.

It wasn't until my husband and I separated and I started to live alone that I had to confront issues almost daily that I had never had to face before. In my new life, if my car needed servicing, I was the one who had to make the appointment and take it in. If an appliance broke, I was the one who got someone out to fix it. If one of my dogs got sick, I was the one who took him to the vet.

Having lived a sheltered and protected life up to that point, I found that my biggest challenge was forcing myself to do something—almost *anything*—for the first time and by myself. I call those experiences "stepping out of my comfort zone." It is still hard for me to do this—it's much easier to sit home on my sofa and click the remote control.

But I have learned that if I can force myself to do something the first time, it gets easier the second, third, and fourth times, etc. For example, when I started to live alone, I had no idea how to pump my own gas. Until then, I had just asked my husband to fill up my car and he did. I mentioned this fear to a very caring friend, and she offered to go with me to the gas station and show me how. The next time I needed gas, I somehow got up enough courage to try it myself. Filling my car with gas that night was the most exciting and freeing experience I have ever had—I was on top of the world! And now, years later, I zip into the gas station and pump gas like an old pro.

So you've been pumping your own gas for years, you say? That's no big deal for you, right? Good for you. But maybe there's something that's hard for you to do that I would find easy—like sending an undercooked steak back to the kitchen or asking a good friend not to smoke in your house. Being courageous means doing the things we're afraid to do *in spite of* our fear. What might take courage for me could be a piece of cake for you, and vice versa. That's o.k.—life is not about comparisons. And we have the right to be very proud of ourselves when we've faced *our* fear and walked through it to the other side.

So—am I courageous? If I use my definition of courage, then yes I am. And I see examples of courage every day: my aunt who cheerfully took care of her double-amputee husband at home by herself the last two years of his life; my cousin's wife who lost her husband and her mother in a period of three weeks; and my dear friend Alice who battled her terminal cancer bravely and with infinite grace.

These are but a few examples—if we look, we can find them all along life's pathway. We don't have to be like Rocky or the Terminator to be courageous.

# Creativity

*Wheresoever you go, go with all your heart.*

—*Anon.*

*To know is nothing at all; to imagine is everything.*

—*Anatole France Thibault*

A women's group I belong to recently spent some time discussing Julia Cameron's book, *The Artist's Way*. At first I couldn't imagine why this would interest me because I'm about as artistic as a telephone pole! But as we delved into the book, I began to understand that there's a difference between being artistic and being creative. No, I'm not artistic and I never will be—I don't paint or sing or dance. But I learned that we are all creative. We were born creative. That's how God intended us to be. We are the ones who build barriers around ourselves that keep us from recognizing and accepting our creativity.

Why would we sabotage ourselves? Cameron suggests we have a lot of garbage running through our heads that keeps us from looking deep within ourselves to discover the creativity we all possess. One of her solutions is to write "morning pages"—three pages in longhand every morning. It doesn't matter what we write—we're not trying to be creative here or write the next best-selling novel. What we're doing is getting rid of all the garbage in our minds so we can uncover the creativity that lies beneath.

So I tried writing morning pages. I even bought her journal to write them in—after all, I am a perfectionist, you know! The first morning I wrote, "I don't know what I'm going to write but I'm going to write BIG!" But I faithfully wrote my three morning pages every day for several months, and I have to admit it did help get rid of the clutter in my head.

And then I stopped writing the pages. I'm not sure why, but I think it might be that I was afraid to discover what was underneath all that clutter.

Why am I so afraid? It's all about allowing myself to be vulnerable and letting others see the real me. What if I tell you who I am and you don't like me—or you don't like what I create? What I am is all I have—so then what? I think I'm scared of all the "what ifs" and second guessing that would follow.

I have another interesting theory: Maybe I'm afraid I *will* succeed! Maybe there really is something wonderful deep within my creative self but because I have such low self-esteem, I don't want to believe it. So I erect a wall around myself by refusing to even try.

I have been told by more than one person that I'm a good writer. I'm not convinced of that—yet. That's why it has been so hard for me to write this book. What if no one likes it? What if it stinks? How will I handle that? Will I say to myself, "I knew I never should have done it—I knew I would be a failure."?

But more and more I'm coming to believe what Julia Cameron says—that we are all creative beings and we must simply dig deep enough into our selves to find that creativity. If that is true, then I have to write. I get excited when I think about writing and my mind is overflowing with ideas all the time. Writing feels right and the words and ideas come from my heart. In the end, isn't that all that matters?

# Do Small Things with Great Love

*What we need is to love without getting tired. How does a lamp burn? Through the continuous input of small drops of oil. What are these drops of oil in our lamps? They are the small things of daily life: faithfulness, small words of kindness, a thought for others, our way of being silent, of looking, of speaking, and of acting.*

—*Mother Teresa*

I believe the world would be a kinder, gentler place if we all took Mother Teresa's advice to heart. Isn't it amazing how the little things we do in life are the ones that always mean the most—to others and to us? And because they are "little things," they usually don't take much time—a smile, a hug, a compliment, a phone call—but what a difference a "little thing" can make in someone else's life. We might never know it but a simple gesture like a hug could change a person's life. I know for sure it will brighten their day.

Sometimes a kind gesture may not take much time but it may take a lot of effort. It's not easy to call or visit a friend who has received bad news—a serious illness, an automobile accident, or losing a loved one, for example. Before I make one of those calls or visits, I try to spend some quiet time with God, asking for His guidance in knowing what words of comfort to offer. I have learned that short of spouting out a bunch of inane clichés, the person who is hurting won't remember what you say but *will* remember that you cared enough to be there for them at a difficult time.

In my mind, Mother Teresa was the epitome of kindness. Humbly and simply with no fanfare, she practiced her ministry of faith and love in the poverty and squalor of Calcutta, India. She sought out those who needed her most: the lepers, the homeless, the dying. Through the Order of Missionaries of Charity which she founded in Calcutta in 1953, she was eventually able to reach out to countless needy people all over the world. How did she practice her faith? By reaching out to those less fortunate, offering them love, kindness, and hope. By reaching out to one downtrodden person at a time. There were skeptics who said she was undertaking a task that was way too big for her—they said she would never succeed. She silenced her critics by making a difference in the lives of many people, one person at a time.

I sometimes wonder what, if anything, my friends and family will remember about me when I'm gone. Perhaps even more important is what I'd *like* for them to remember. I don't want them to remember the long hours I had to work at certain times in my career, but I do want them to know that I love what I'm doing now—so much so that I can't wait to get to work every day! I hope they don't remember the times I lost my temper and got angry, but I hope they will remember the times I was there for them—with a hug, a kind word, or perhaps just a listening ear. I hope they don't remember all those years I spent living in a fog, but rather I hope they remember the years after I woke up—I hope they can appreciate how far I've come and understand how much courage it has taken.

How would I like to be remembered? I would like my epitaph to simply read: "She did small things with great love."

# Friendship

*I would not live without the love of my friends.*

*—Keats*

*If a man does not make new acquaintances as he advances through life, he will soon find himself alone. A man, sir, must keep his friendships in current repair.*

*—Johnson*

Soon after that day when my life changed forever and I was forced to come out of the fog I had lived in for years, my therapist urged me to talk about everything that was happening to me with a good friend. I literally cringed when he said that because I couldn't imagine sharing all that pain and humiliation with another person. Besides, I knew my close friends were dealing with a lot of "stuff" in their lives and the last thing I wanted to do was add to their burdens. Finally, I was afraid if I actually talked about my situation, that would make it real. Somehow I was still hoping it was just a bad dream and that it would go away if I ignored it.

But my therapist was pretty persistent—he felt strongly that I needed to talk to a caring friend. So I did. My friend and I spent a Saturday afternoon together about a week later. I shall be forever grateful to her for the time she spent with me that day and for her love, concern, and compassion.

What an amazing afternoon it was! I learned so many lessons that day. First, I found out it wasn't nearly as hard to share my innermost thoughts as I had feared. Of course, it was very important to share them with a compassionate friend who wouldn't judge me or tell me what to do. Sharing my feelings somehow "normalized" my situation a bit—it didn't seem quite so dire once I was able to talk about it.

Another valuable lesson I learned that day is that friendship is a two-way street. We didn't spend every minute talking about me and my situation. We also talked about my friend and what was going on in her life. So it was a win-win situation: she was there for me and I was there for her, and both of us knew our burdens were lighter at the end of the day because of the love and concern we shared.

From that day on, our friendship has grown and blossomed and become deeper and deeper. I am lucky to have such a special friend and I know she feels the same way.,

My Psych 101 professor in college (an all-girl's school) told us to cultivate and cherish our friendships with other women because they would remain the one constant in our lives over the years. I've always remembered that advice—how right she was! My husband is long gone and a lot of my worldly possessions disappeared with the dissolution of the marriage. But I'm still alive and kicking—and doing very well, thank you!—due in no small part to the love and support I've received from several good friends who have stuck by me through it all.

A very important word in my professor's advice is "cultivate." Like all relationships, friendships must be cultured and nurtured. It's also important to realize that there may be times when we're closer to our friends than others. Because all our lives are constantly changing, we may need to go our separate ways for a while. During those times, it's important to be able to talk about how we feel. True friendships can usually survive these ebbs and flows but only if we are able to keep the lines of communication open and express our feelings honestly.

Because of these ebbs and flows, it's also very important to continue to seek out new friends. If we don't, we could find ourselves alone and lonely, depending on what's going on in our friends' lives at the moment. If we are introverts or if we are dealing with self-esteem issues, reaching out to others may not be easy. It never is for me. Even though I know it's not necessarily true, I still cringe when I invite someone to do something with me and they decline because they say they have other plans. Even after all these years of working on my self-esteem issues, I'm totally convinced the real reason they're saying "no" is because they don't like me and they don't want to spend time with me. Then I have to spend a lot of time *forcing* myself to erase those old tapes and constantly *reinforcing* my belief that I am a loved and loving person.

I must admit that I sometimes "cheat" when I get ready to ask someone to do something—I often do it by e-mail or voicemail! For some reason, knowing that I won't get an immediate response makes it easier for me to muster enough courage to issue the invitation. I'm not saying this is the best way to develop new friendships, but for me it's a good solution to a difficult situation. What is important is that no matter how hard it is for me, I continue to make the effort to reach out to others. And for that effort, I have been richly rewarded with some special friendships.

I can count on my fingers the number of true friends I have. Each of them is a blessing in my life and all of them have a special place in my heart.

# Healing Past Wounds

*Everyone is the Child of his past.*

—*Edna G. Rostow*

*Even God cannot change the past.*

—*Agathon*

We humans are complicated creatures, comprised of many parts. All the experiences we've had during our lifetime combine to create the person we are right now, especially those experiences occurring during our childhood years. I have attended enough 12-step meetings to know how deeply our childhood memories affect us as adults. Many times they remain unresolved well into adulthood (in fact, some people never resolve them) and we remain stuck in whichever defense mechanism we unconsciously choose (denial, anger, acting out, etc.)

I am amazed that siblings reared in the same household can have completely different perceptions of their childhood years. It certainly happened in my family. Many times my brother and I would have a completely different take on a situation we both experienced. And interestingly, his take was almost always more positive than mine.

What intrigues me is how two people living in the same environment and involved in the same episode can have such different opinions about what happened. Is it because one is in denial and the other is facing the truth? Is it because we played different roles in our family? Or is it just that one sees the glass half full and the other sees it half empty? There's no "right" or "wrong" answer, of course, but it's fascinating to look at the apparent disparities that often exist between, and even among, siblings.

Since all our prior experiences are so much a part of who we are now, I think it's important to spend some time trying to make sense of what happened during our childhood years, especially if we were abused in any way while we were growing up (and remember, abuse can be emotional as well as physical). I was able to examine many of my childhood issues in 12-step meetings, in individual therapy, and by journaling. It was very important for me to be able to write and talk about my childhood years in order to get a better idea of the part they played in making me who I am today.

At some point, it was also very important for me to be able to let go of the past and start living in the present. But I never could have done that without first exploring my past and facing my own personal demons. Then and only then could I honestly tell myself that I had dealt with the past and that I could put it behind me and move on. It's important to be able to do this at some point, although it may take a while to get there. If we can't let go of the past, then we're still using a defense mechanism and we'll be forever stuck.

# Laughter

*There aren't many things as therapeutic as smiles and laughter. Whenever you look at things in a lighter vein, it shows that your heart is in the right place.*

—*Douglas Pagels*

*Everyone smiles in the same language.*

—*Proverb*

Thank you, "Wings," Dave Barry, and Biscuit and Rascal for saving my life, not once but many times!

I first experienced the healing power of laughter the day my former husband and I signed our arbitration agreement and he left town. I was devastated—so much so that I wasn't sure whether I could drive myself home. But I made it, and after spending some time outside with my dogs, I turned on the TV just as the sitcom "Wings" was coming on. It was one of my favorite shows because it always made me laugh. Before I knew it, the show was over and an entire half hour had gone by—a half hour in which I wasn't depressed or feeling sorry for myself but was instead totally involved in watching a funny TV show. Imagine that—in the midst of all my pain and sadness, I was actually laughing out loud!

Dave Barry is one of my favorite people on the planet. He's the Pulitzer-Prize-winning humor columnist at the *Miami Herald*. I can't wait to read his column every week—he keeps me in stitches and often makes me laugh out loud. What a gift he has and how glad I am that he shares his gift with all of us.

My two golden retrievers have kept me alive and sane through all the peaks and valleys of my life during the last 12 years, simply by always being there for me. They let me feel all my feelings—and they, too, often make me laugh out loud.

When I teach classes on grief, I always discuss the topic, "Healing through Laughter and Tears." Both laughter and tears are wonderful tools to help us through our grief. Usually the tears come first—and it's very important to give ourselves permission to cry and feel our pain. The laughter will usually come later, although sometimes tears and laughter come at the same time. Think about it—what happens when we lose a loved one? Friends and family gather around us as we grieve (and if you live in the South like I do, they always bring lots of delicious food!). Of course we're sad and we shed lots of tears. But have you noticed that we also laugh a lot? Someone will start reminiscing about the loved one who died and will tell a funny story and before you know it, we're laughing and remembering the happy times too.

Both tears and laughter are extremely therapeutic as we go through any grieving process. Have you ever noticed how much better you feel after you've had a good cry? And once you're able to laugh at a situation, it's never as serious or sad as it was before. Laughter helps us put things in perspective.

Back to "Wings"—when we're laughing, really laughing, we are living completely in the present moment. We're not rehashing the past or worrying about the future—we're totally in the "now."

Laughter is a precious gift from God—use it often!

# *Listening*

*We have two ears but only one mouth, that we may hear more and speak less.*

—*Zeno*

*No man would listen to you talk if he didn't know it was his turn next.*

—*Ed Howe*

One of the classes we teach in Stephen Ministry training is how to become an active listener. Trust me—it's not easy! Being an active listener takes concentration, energy, and hard work.

Here are some ways to become a better listener:

- *Really* listen. This means tuning out everything else that's going on in your life and focusing totally on what the other person is saying.

- Be compassionate. Realize that it is never easy for someone to share their personal feelings with another person, so treat this as a sacred trust.

- Be non-judgmental and neutral, both in what you say and how you act. Make sure you don't express shock or disgust at what you're hearing.

- Listen with your "third" ear. In addition to what is being said (or not said), pay attention to physical characteristics like facial expressions, changes in the tone of voice, body movements (wringing the hands, etc.), eye contact or lack of it, nervous laughter, etc.

- Don't offer advice or try to "fix" it. Even if you're sure you know what the other person should do, don't tell them! At some point in the conversation, you may want to *suggest* a solution ("Have you thought about…?") but remember, it's up to the other person to decide whether or not to act on your suggestion.

All Stephen Ministers make a commitment to spend an average of one hour each week visiting with their care receiver. Our Stephen Ministers often say to me, "I don't feel like I'm doing my care receiver any good—all I'm doing is listening to him (or her)."

And I say to them, "Do you have any idea how many people want and need someone to simply listen to them, especially if they know that person isn't going to judge them or tell them what they should do? In this crazy world we live in, do you know what a gift it is to give someone an hour of your undivided attention each week?"

Never underestimate the value of being a caring, active listener!

# Patience

*Have patience with all things but first of all with yourself.*

—*Saint Francis of Sales*

What's the first thing we usually do when something goes wrong? We panic! It's like a knee-jerk reaction, a conditioned reflex. We forget to set our alarm clock and oversleep—we panic. Our car won't start—we panic. Our boss needs three reports for a meeting that has already started—we panic.

Yet losing our cool is the worst thing we can do. It keeps us from being able to think logically and when we can't do that, we actually add to our panic.

When something like this happens to me, I do my best to stay calm. Taking some deep breaths helps. Realizing I can't control what has happened helps. What helps most is to calmly try to figure out what needs to be done and go about making that happen.

For example, I went out to go to work one morning recently and my neighbor came over to tell me I had a flat tire. The first thing I did was panic, thinking things like, "Oh no, I'm going to be late for work." and "How am I going to get my tire fixed?" But after thinking irrationally for a couple of minutes, I calmed down and began to figure out what I needed to do—call my automobile club and get someone out to fix my tire, call my office and tell them I would be late, etc. Once I had a plan, I was fine. I had moved from a state of panic to a state of action.

At some point, I actually started to feel grateful. That might sound strange, but I realized that a flat tire wasn't such a big deal in the whole scheme of things. I was grateful I had been able to take care of getting it fixed fairly easily, and I was grateful to my neighbor for telling me my tire was flat so I didn't end up driving on it and ruining the tire. The point is that I could not have experienced those feelings of gratitude when I was in a panic, so I was also grateful I had figured out how to move out of the panic mode and into the action mode.

You see, these little annoyances are going to happen to us from time to time whether we like it or not. It's how we deal with them that's important. In this fast-paced world we live in, we'll function much more rationally and much less stressfully if we can master the calming virtue of patience.

# Possessions

*In this world there are only two tragedies. One is not getting what one wants, and the other is getting it.*

*—Oscar Wilde*

*You can't have everything. Where would you put it?*

*—Steven Wright*

Rabbi Harold Kushner has written several excellent books, and one of my favorites is *When All You've Ever Wanted Isn't Enough—The Search for a Life That Matters*. In an effort to help his readers discover the real meaning of their lives, he spends a lot of time exploring and interpreting the Book of Ecclesiastes. This Book was written by someone nearing the end of his life who questions the value of his life and wonders whether or not he has made a difference in this world.

I can empathize with the author of Ecclesiastes. I have talked to therapists and friends alike about what I call the "hole in my soul." I keep trying to fill it with "things" but no matter how many things I put in it, the hole in my soul won't go away. And the joy I experience when I try to fill it is fleeting.

I have figured it out intellectually—I just haven't been able to embrace it with my heart yet. I heard someone say once that the distance between our head and our heart is less than one foot—why does it often take so long for knowledge to travel from one to the other?

This much I know: as long as I'm depending on other people or my possessions to bring meaning to my life, I am doomed. People die, spouses leave, friends come and go—so if I'm counting on any of them to fulfill me and bring me everlasting joy, I am in deep trouble. That big job I landed paying huge bucks could be eliminated next week. In which case, that big boat and fancy car I bought to impress all my friends can be repossessed in the blink of an eye.

And does it really matter how many pairs of shoes I have? After all, I can't wear but one pair at a time! Then why do I keep buying them? Do I think people will like me better if I have more shoes? Or more sweaters? Or more books and collectibles? With whom am I trying to compete to see who has the most things? Am I still trying to convince myself I can survive on my own and buying things is my way of proving that to myself? Or do I just get a temporary high while I'm buying something even though I often lose interest in it before I take it out of the shopping bag? I imagine it's a combination of all these things and probably others as well.

What the author of Ecclesiastes came to realize late in his life is what I'm trying so desperately to accept in my heart right now. You see, it's not about the clothes we wear or the job we have or the car we drive. It's not about anything that can be taken away from us. It's about our relationship with ourselves and our Higher Power. It's about living in the "now"—dealing with the past and putting it behind us, and refusing to get caught up in the "what ifs" about the future. It's about getting up every morning with the hope that we can in some small way make a positive difference in someone else's life. It's about giving each day all we've got—at work, at home, at play, at church. It's about knowing that every day is a gift from God and trying to live it as if it were our last day on earth. Once we realize this, our lives become quite simple, really—and we are filled with an incredible sense of peace.

# Receiving and Giving

*One can never pay in gratitude; one can only pay in kind somewhere else in life.*

—*Anne Morrow Lindbergh*

How many times have I heard someone say, "It is more blessed to give than to receive."? I don't subscribe to that theory—at least not always.

Life is like a pendulum, always swinging back and forth depending on what we're experiencing at any given time. There are times when we want to—and can—give something back. And there are times when we need to receive from others.

And let me tell you this: it is ever so much easier to give than to receive. I am in no way diminishing the act of giving. It is an act of love and it is an honorable thing to do. But to realize we need help and to ask for it requires an incredible amount of wisdom and courage. It is sad that many people think asking for help is a sign of weakness. Absolutely not—it is a sign of great courage!

And guess what? If you allow yourself to be a gracious receiver, you will be a better giver. It's true! Think about it. Why is it so hard for some of us to accept a compliment or a gift? Why do we often try to negate the compliment or return the gift ("This old dress? I've had it for years and it's completely out of style.") Whatever our reasons are for being an ungracious receiver (low self-esteem, always a caregiver, etc.), we demean not only ourselves but also the giver. We are sending the message to the giver that he/she isn't sincere and that we are unworthy.

So accept those compliments and gifts because you deserve them. Don't try to give them back or qualify them. Just say a simple "thank you" and be done with it. Being on the receiving end a few times will help you understand what that feels like and you'll be a better giver because of it.

# *Small Steps*

*The smallest action is greater than the finest intention.*

*—Anon.*

Have you ever felt totally overwhelmed by all the things you have to do? I know I have. After my mother died, I would sit in my living room thinking about everything I needed to do. In addition to my own responsibilities, I was also having to deal with all the legal matters regarding her estate. I didn't have the energy to do anything about any of it, mind you—so I just sat on my sofa doing nothing and feeling guilty about all the things I *should* be doing.

There's a good chance we'll all feel overwhelmed at some point in our lives, probably more than once. One way to tackle those seemingly insurmountable tasks is to break them down into smaller, more manageable segments by using the small-step approach. Here's how it works:

Suppose my house is a total wreck and I have decided I can't live with all this junk any more. Why can't I just say to myself that I'm going to clean it from top to bottom this weekend, even if it kills me?

Because taking on a mammoth chore like cleaning my whole house is way too big a job for me to bite off at one time. Telling myself I'm going to get it spotless in a weekend is setting myself up for failure and disappointment.

On the other hand, I might be able to tackle one room—or one closet—or the drawers in one dresser. You get the idea. By breaking this task down into several smaller, more manageable segments, there is a much better chance I'll reach my goal. It's important to set a goal you can accomplish—it's much more rewarding to be able to check a small task off your list than not to complete a large, unmanageable one.

Another way to tackle a huge task is to set aside a certain amount of time each day—or each week—to work on it, making sure you have a reasonable time frame in which you want to complete the whole project. Instead of saying you're going to clean an entire room, you might say you're going to spend an hour every other night cleaning your house until you have completed your task but that you will finish it within a month.

The important thing is to set attainable goals with a specific, realistic time frame.

# *Spontaneity*

*Not a shred of evidence exists in favor of the idea that life is serious.*

—*Brendan Gill*

Why do I think life has to be so rigid and predictable? Why don't I laugh more often? Why can't I take a chance every once in a while even if it doesn't work out?

There are several reasons, of course. I'm a control freak so I'm most comfortable when everything goes the way I want it to. It's hard for me to leave my comfort zone and take a chance because I'm so afraid I'll fail or that I'll look stupid. And perhaps there weren't many times in the past when I felt like laughing.

It has only been in recent years that I realized I have a dry sense of humor. Maybe it's because I'm able to laugh at myself now. Sometimes when I'm in a bad place emotionally or when there's a task I need to get done that's impossible for me to do by myself, I'll freak out and start yelling and screaming. In and of itself, that's not a bad thing. In fact, it's very healthy to yell and scream. But it does spook my dogs! They usually run to another room and hide until I calm down. Then they'll peep around the corner to check on me and make sure it's o.k. for them to come back. That always cracks me up so I start laughing at them and all of a sudden my situation doesn't seem nearly so serious or unattainable as it did 30 minutes earlier.

Learning to be more flexible has also helped me be more spontaneous. Realizing that I'm not in charge of my life has taken a huge weight off my shoulders and has truly set me free. Now that I don't have to plan every move I make, complete with Plans B, C, and D, it's easier for me to be more flexible and even take a risk now and then.

Now that I'm not a kid any more, I have a sense of urgency about getting on with whatever it is I want to do with my life. I've been thinking about writing this book for a couple of years, but I just recently decided it was time to get serious and make that dream a reality. Knowing that I don't have as many years ahead of me as I have already lived motivates me to search deep into my heart to find those special things that give me pleasure and joy and make them part of my life every single day. And since none of us knows how long we'll live, that seems to be a wonderful goal for all of us, no matter what our chronological age might be.

# Taking a Risk

*"How does one become a butterfly?" she asked pensively. "You must want to fly so much that you are willing to give up being a caterpillar."*

—Trina Paulus, <u>Hope for the Flowers</u>

*There is nothing in a caterpillar that tells you it's going to be a butterfly.*

—Buckminster Fuller

Oh how comfortable it is in my cocoon! I feel safe and warm and content. I never want to leave it! Or do I? Do I sometimes feel a little bit restricted in such a small space? And is "safe and warm and content" all I want out of my life?

For many years it was. My life was out of control in so many ways that I clung to the familiar much longer than I should have. My marriage was falling apart and I didn't like my job, but I didn't want to do anything to rock the boat because at least I knew what to expect from both of them.

Why did I hold on for so long? Why did I practically ruin my mental and emotional health before I did something? Because I was afraid—no, terrified—of the unknown. All those "what if" questions kept running through my mind. What if my marriage ended and I had to survive on my own? For someone who was afraid to spend a night alone, this was more than a fear, it was a full-blown phobia. What if I lost my job, even though I didn't particularly like it? How would I survive, especially if my marriage was also in jeopardy? What if, what if, WHAT IF??!!

Thinking back on those empty years, I realize another reason I held on for so long was because I thought I deserved my life. After all, I had never been able to live up to my expectations of myself, so in my mind my marriage and my job were just two more ways I had failed. It was all my fault, I assured myself. If only I were smarter, thinner, funnier, prettier, more efficient—*ad nauseum*—I could make my marriage and my job work. If only, if only, IF ONLY!!

And then one sunny February day, my world as I knew it fell apart when my husband sat me down and told me some things that changed my life forever.

What he told me doesn't matter—what matters is what happened to me from that day on—and how I managed to survive. Somehow, I knew right away that I could no longer live in denial—that I must face each day head-on for the first time in my life. I was terrified. All my fears were going to come true—my marriage was falling apart, I would have to survive on my own, I would have to spend every night alone. How was I going to do it? *Could* I do it? I didn't think I could.

Coming out of denial and into the real world was a lot like spending many years in a windowless basement and then suddenly coming out into the bright sunshine. The change was blinding and I was paralyzed with fear. How could I face each day with no crutches to help me through? I had no idea.

How did I do it? Slowly—very slowly—one day at a time. My journey from cocoon to butterfly was so gradual that I often couldn't see any progress at all. Sometimes I took two steps forward and one step backward—but I persevered and after a while, I began to have a glimmer of hope. Slowly but surely I began to emerge from my cocoon. And once you become a butterfly, you shed your cocoon for good.

# Tolerance

*I disapprove of what you say, but I will defend to the death your right to say it.*

*—Voltaire*

*A major advantage of age is learning to accept people without passing judgment.*

*—Liz Carpenter*

Tolerance is more important today than it has ever been. In an age when we can communicate with someone halfway around the globe in literally an instant via e-mail or the Web, our world, with all its diversity, seems to be shrinking every day.

I was in a training class composed of all women several years ago and the topic was tolerance (and prejudice, its opposite). Four intelligent women led the discussion that night and while I've forgotten exactly what they said, I won't ever forget the impression they made on me and how they changed my views about tolerance and prejudice.

You see, at the end of the class, each of them told us a little bit about themselves, and some of what they said surprised us. One woman with blonde hair told us she was Jewish and another woman told us she was a lesbian. They definitely weren't the stereotypical Jewish or gay person and until then, none of us had any idea as to who these people were and what their backgrounds were. Would we have treated them differently if we had known more about them? Possibly.

The point they were trying to emphasize was that all of us prejudge people by what they look like, how they talk, what they do for a living, etc. It's so easy to do—we "pigeon-hole" someone into a category—Jewish, gay, black, white, rich, poor, smart, stupid—before we know anything about them. We don't give them a chance because we have already made up our minds as to whether or not we like them.

Tolerance is all about accepting and respecting the behavior and opinions of others, whether or not we agree with them. Prejudice, on the other hand, is about having a preconceived idea or preference about someone's behavior and opinions. We close our minds and make a snap judgment before we know all the facts.

There will always be people in our lives whom we like more than others—that's just human nature. But it is important for us to take the time to get to know people before we make hasty decisions about whether or not we like them. This in no way means we can't have our own opinions and feelings—it just means we become open-minded enough to accept the opinions and feelings of others even when they differ from ours.

What would happen if *all* of us were more accepting of *everyone*? What if each one of us made a concerted effort to accept others, whether or not they were like us? We would have a kinder, gentler planet on which to live and learn and grow.

Think about it: what if they gave a war and nobody came? It's up to each one of us to do our part in making that question a reality.

# *Worry*

*Happy is the man who has broken the chains which hurt the mind, and has given up worrying once and for all.*

—*Ovid*

*Worrying does not empty tomorrow of its troubles—it empties today of its strength.*

—*Anon.*

I have always been a worrier, so much so that I actually used to think I could control the outcome of a situation by how much I worried. I figured the more I worried about something, the better the chance was that it would turn out like I wanted it to. Conversely, when I wasn't worrying about something, I felt guilty. What if something bad happened and I hadn't worried about it? Then I would be partially responsible, right?

So exactly when did I appoint myself God? I am giving myself way too much power if I think I can control the outcome of what happens in a particular situation. It all comes back to control—somehow I think I can control it by worrying about it. WRONG!

I learned a valuable lesson about worrying a few years ago when I had tear duct replacement surgery for the second time. I had had the same surgery in my other eye several years earlier and it had been pretty traumatic, but for some reason I wasn't worried about the second operation. Maybe it was because I thought I knew what to expect. At any rate, I was able to stay in the moment, trust my surgeon and God (not necessarily in that order!) and not worry—a huge accomplishment for me! As it turns out, the surgery went fine but I had a reaction to the anesthesia. What should have been out-patient surgery ended up being a three-day hospital stay because I fainted every time I sat up or stood up!

Here's what I learned from this experience: no matter how many things I could have worried about, it never would have crossed my mind to worry about having an allergic reaction to the anesthesia. So I saved myself a lot of time and energy by not worrying about *anything*.

Worrying is an incredible waste of time and emotional energy. It never changes anything and it's such exhausting work. Not worrying is about having faith and living in the moment.

Did you know that almost everything you worry about never comes true? And no, the outcome is not affected by whether or not you worry!

There's a cute Peanuts book by Charles Schultz called *Me, Stressed Out?* In that book, Charlie Brown wakes up in the middle of the night and says, "It's very strange…sometimes you lie in bed at night and you don't have a single thing to worry about…that always worries me!"

What would happen if we didn't worry? We'd be free to live our lives without fear; we'd be able to live in the "now" and leave the rest to God; and we'd be at peace with ourselves. Even though it's not easy, I try to enjoy each day as it unfolds and let tomorrow take care of itself when it becomes today.

# Living peacefully...

# Balance

*Maintain a good balance. A personal life adds dimensions to your professional life and vice versa. It helps nurture creativity through a deeper understanding of yourself.*

—Kathy Ireland

*Each day, and the living of it, has to be a conscious creation in which discipline and order are relieved with some play and pure foolishness.*

—May Sarton

Finding balance is hard if you're an addict, a codependent, or a perfectionist. When you're all three like I am, it is definitely an uphill battle.

If you're an addict, you simply have two choices: to abstain or to use. Addiction isn't about finding balance within the addiction—it's about making a conscious decision to use or not to use—and sometimes you must make that decision many times each day. I've known alcoholics who went to five or more AA meetings a day to try to stay sober.

Codependents also have trouble finding balance. We try so hard to take care of everyone else that we neglect ourselves. Or we spend all our time and energy doing volunteer work and then feel guilty because we're too exhausted to spend time with family and friends. Or we work 80 hours a week slaving away at our job and then wonder why we don't have the energy to go to our son's soccer game or sing in the choir.

Perfectionists often struggle with balance too. We want to do everything perfectly or we don't want to do it at all. I'm sure that's why I sit on my sofa and work crossword puzzles so often instead of cleaning my house or doing other chores I need to do. Crossword puzzles are my ultimate cop-out!

Moderation is a virtue I very much admire but know I will never possess. My mother was always able to act moderately—she could eat one piece of cake and stop, she could have one drink and stop, she could go shopping and buy one thing and stop. The key here is that she could have done without all of these things and she would have been fine. I clearly didn't inherit her genes!

But even though I know I must be ever vigilant in dealing with my addictions, there are other areas in my life where I can strive for balance and moderation. First and foremost, I must make a conscious decision to take care of myself. I must erase the old tapes telling me it's selfish to put myself first. I must replace them with new ones telling me it's vital to my physical, mental, and emotional well-being to put myself first.

Another area where we need to find balance is in our profession. We spend a lot of time at work and it's easy to get so totally wrapped up in our career that it becomes who we are. How many times has someone asked us, "What do you do?" as if that defines who we are. While I think it's very important to enjoy what we do for a living, it's also important to realize that it's just a job and it's just a segment of our life and who we are.

I once spent some time with a very wise counselor when I was at a crossroads in my career. My job at that time wasn't very fulfilling and I kept thinking there was something else I wanted—and needed—to do with my life. After discussing the pros and cons of several options, my counselor told me it is rare that some-one's vocation and avocation are the same. Most people have a vocation that sup-ports them so they can indulge in the avocation of their choice. So she and I tried to find some of the ways I could pursue my dreams through an avocation.

I'm happy to say I have a different job (vocation) now, which I love. But I refuse to let it consume me, and I try very hard to have enough time and energy left over for my avocation, as well as for my hobbies, my family and friends, my church, and—most importantly—myself.

For me, balance is all about being in control of myself and my time. It's about finding out what's important to me and making sure I have the time to do those things which bring me joy. It's also about being able to say "no" to those things I don't want to do so I can say "yes" to those I do. It's about realizing I can't do everything and I can't please everyone, so I must always be making choices. It's about realizing that when *my* well is dry, I am of no use to myself or anyone else.

And most importantly for me, it's about understanding that when there is bal-ance in my life and when I'm doing things I enjoy and that make me happy, I'm able to do those things better because I have stopped doing everything for every-body and started doing what matters most to me.

# *Gratitude*

*Thou hast given so much to me...Give one thing more—a grateful heart.*

—*George Herbert*

*Gratitude makes sense of our past, brings peace for today, and creates a vision for tomorrow.*

—*Melody Beattie*

Soon after emerging from my fog, I kept seeing in the word "gratitude" in Melody Beattie's books and I was baffled. She was saying we should be grateful for everything that happens to us, whether or not we think it's a good thing at the time.

How can that be? Oh, I know it's easy to be grateful for the good things that happen to us—finding that special person with whom we want to share our life, getting that job we've wanted so desperately, buying the house of our dreams, and so on. I can see where I wouldn't have a problem being grateful for things like that.

But the problem was that I didn't have any of those things in my life right then. In fact, I was hard-pressed to think of anything I could be grateful for. But if I understood what Beattie was saying, I was supposed to be grateful for exactly what was happening to me in my life at that very minute.

Did she mean I was supposed to be grateful that my marriage had broken up, that I had to live alone, that I was the sole breadwinner, and that I had to do everything around my house if it got done at all? And how, exactly, was I supposed to go about that? I'm talking about being honestly grateful, not just mouthing the words.

I must confess it took me a long time before I understood what gratitude is all about. You see, what happens in my life at any given time is part of God's plan for me. I'm not supposed to question why certain things happen when they do—what I need to do is figure out the best way to deal with them. And I have found that my greatest growth and wisdom have come from the difficult times I've experienced—the very ones I didn't want to happen at all.

No, I didn't want my marriage to break up. I wanted to grow old with my spouse—or so I thought at the time. I didn't want to live alone—I was terrified to be by myself at night. And I surely didn't want to be completely responsible for my financial needs at this point in my life. When I got married, I figured that was the end of my financial worries!

But these things did happen, and I am a better, stronger, and more compassionate person for having dealt with them. I have learned more about myself and others in the last few years than I learned in all my years before then. There's something powerful about dealing with difficult issues and coming through them intact. You find out you're stronger than you imagined and you become empowered with the strength and courage you need to tackle whatever happens next.

There are so many things that have happened in my life in the last few years—both large and small—that I never dreamed I could deal with, much less deal with *well*. I know, of course, that I didn't deal with them alone—God was with me all the time, saying "you can do it, my child, you can do it—I am always with you."

Maybe I didn't *want* to experience a lot of the things I've been through, but I know now that I *needed* to experience every one of them in order to grow, to have the courage to come out of my cocoon, and to have more compassion for others.

If that's what gratitude is all about, then I'm grateful for it every day of my life.

# *Nature*

*The sun, with all those planets revolving around it and dependent on it, can still ripen a bunch of grapes as if it had nothing else in the universe to do.*

—*Galileo*

*Live in each season as it passes; breathe the air, drink the drink, taste the fruit, and resign yourself to the influences of each.*

—*John Muir*

My mother told me many times she didn't know how anyone could *not* believe in God in the springtime when evidences of His love and majesty are everywhere for us to behold.

The beauty and simplicity of nature can soothe and calm us. A brisk walk on a crisp, sunny day is one of the best ways to clear the cobwebs from our heads and hearts. Taking deep breaths along the way and enjoying Mother Nature's bountiful gifts can help ease the turmoil in our souls.

I remember stopping on the sidewalk one day and noticing a huge leaf that had fallen on the ground. It occurred to me that I had been down this same path many times before and had never noticed this tree with its enormous leaves. It made me sad in a way—to know I had never stopped to look at the tree before. It also made me wonder how many other things I've missed out on, either by living in a fog or by being too preoccupied with other things to live in the moment and appreciate all of nature's gifts.

One thing I love about nature is that it's so predictable. In my part of the country, there are four distinct seasons, so I know without a doubt that the magnificent fall foliage will give way to the pristine whiteness of winter's snows. And just when I've had my fill of ice and snow, up pops a daffodil to remind me that spring is just around the corner. To some extent, my moods are affected by the seasons. I'm often listless and apathetic in the heat and humidity of summer and I'm somewhat of a hermit during the long winter months. But I've learned to enjoy each season for its uniqueness. Being a hermit in the winter is fine with me because it gives me an excuse to spend a lazy afternoon lying on the couch reading a good book, warm and toasty in front of a crackling fire.

If you really want to experience the joys of nature up close, take a dog for a walk! My golden retriever can spend 30 minutes walking around a single block as he stops to sniff and examine what must be every leaf and stick on the ground! Seeing nature's bounty through his eyes gives me an even deeper appreciation of it.

When I am attuned to nature, I am at peace with myself and all of God's creations. Those are the special times when I agree with Robert Browning when he wrote:

"God's in His Heaven, all's right with the world,..."

# New Beginnings

*Each new day is a gift from God. How you live it is your gift to Him.*

—Anon.

*I know not what the future holds,*
*but I know who holds the future.*

—Anon.

I remember vividly the time between Christmas and New Year's the year we separated and I moved into my own place. I couldn't *wait* for the old year to end and the new year to begin. It had been a difficult and emotionally draining year and I was ready for it to be over.

Imagine my total surprise when New Year's Day finally arrived and nothing had changed! For some reason, I thought I could sit back and do nothing and everything would be all better on January 1. I wish it were that easy but that's just not the way it works.

Life is a continuous journey and we must be a willing participant in it. If we sit around idly waiting for the next Monday or the next month or the next year to roll around in hopes that a date on the calendar will magically improve our present situation, we're in for a lot of disappointments.

I do like to spend some time at the end of each year documenting what I've done that year and making a list of what I'd like to accomplish in the year ahead. I don't make New Year's resolutions because I don't seem to be able to keep them, which depresses me and makes my new year start off on the wrong foot. Instead, I try to set several attainable goals for the coming year. And it's empowering for me to review the old year to see what kind of progress I've made and whether or not I've accomplished the goals I set for myself.

But it's also important for me to remember that *any* day can be a new beginning. For that matter, *any* time during any day can be a new beginning. I don't need to wait for some artificial time period (the first of the year, month, week, etc.) to start making changes in my life. Someone once told me he was going to

113

go on a diet, stop smoking, and stop drinking the following Monday. Talk about setting himself up for failure! He was back to all three of his old habits by the end of the first week.

God gives us our life one day at a time and it's all we're promised. Only when we can begin to fill each day with the things that bring us happiness will we start to experience His love and grace that is always there for us.

# *Success*

To laugh often and love much;
To win the respect of intelligent persons and the
affection of children;
to earn the approbation of honest citizens and endure
the betrayal of false friends;
to appreciate beauty;
to find the best in others;
to give of one's self;
to leave the world a bit better, whether by a healthy
child, a garden patch or a redeemed social condition;
to have played and laughed with enthusiasm and sung
with exultation;
to know even one life has breathed easier because you
have lived—
this is to have succeeded.

*—Ralph Waldo Emerson*

*(There are no words I could pen that would come close to the beauty of this definition of success from one of our country's most beloved poets so I'm not even going to try.)*

# *Pets*

*I believe animals have been talking to human beings since we were all made and put into this world.*

*—Barbara Woodhouse*

*Dogs are children that are never quite able to grow up, no matter how smart they are. And so they always make us feel important and needed. We are. We always have our place with them. And we know what that place is, in contrast to our relationship with many of the members of our own species that we encounter in life.*

*—Roger Caras*

This writing will come at the end of my little book and it's also the last piece I will write. Pets have always been an integral part of my life and that has made this a hard piece to write.

I'm writing this in honor and in memory of all the pets who have faithfully and lovingly let me share their lives. Their names appear at the end. But most especially, I dedicate this piece to the memory of Biscuit, my beloved golden retriever who died not long ago.

Biscuit and Rascal were a Christmas gift to me from my then-husband. They were littermates and they came to live with us on Christmas Eve when they were six weeks old. If there's anything more precious than two golden retriever puppies, I don't know what it could be! They were two balls of fur and they stole my heart for good that Christmas Eve so many years ago.

People who didn't know them asked me how I could tell them apart. It was very easy for me. Biscuit was leaner and lankier—he really looked like an Irish setter—and he was exceptionally bright. Rascal, on the other hand, was the perfect example of what a golden retriever should look and act like. He was gentle and loving, although sometimes he *did* live up to his name!

And how they loved each other! For almost 12 years they were inseparable. And then the unthinkable happened. Biscuit, who had always been a very healthy dog, began to have seizures. And when he had seven in less than 24 hours, my vet and I knew what had to be done. I had to give my precious dog a final gift—I agreed to let my vet put him to sleep so he would be out of pain and whole again.

For all of you who have pets or love animals, I'm sure you know this was one of the most difficult and saddest days of my life. Intellectually I knew I did the right thing—the only thing—but emotionally I was devastated. I wanted Biscuit back—well and healthy—and I wanted him to live another 25 years at least.

All pet owners know that the odds are we'll eventually lose them unless they should happen to outlive us. I knew this and I honestly thought I was at least somewhat prepared for it. Not in my wildest imagination did I realize how painful it would actually be.

You see, pets occupy a special place in our hearts that no human can ever fill. When Biscuit died, he took a huge piece of my heart with him and I know I'll never be the same again.

Pets love us unconditionally and they ask for so little in return—food and water, shelter, and lots of love. They are always a constant in the craziness that is our life. They don't care how we look, what kind of day we've had, or what we're wearing—they love us just the same. They're always there for us when we unlock the door and come home—happy and excited to see us, wagging their tails like crazy and shaking all over with joy. It's no wonder we love them so much!

I have said in other sections of this book that I'm convinced my dogs saved my life more than once. They were with me during some of the most tumultuous—and later wonderful—years of my life. They were around when I came out of the fog and started to live again. There were times during that transitional period when I'm not sure I would have survived had it not been for them. So in a very real way I owe them my life.

So to my precious Biscuit, I say, "Rest in peace, my sweet puppy dog—you were one of the best." And to my Rascal, I say, "Thank you for still being there for me—we'll help each other through our grief."

And here are the names of all the pets I've had in my lifetime (or at least all the ones my brother and I can remember)—if I've forgotten any of you, forgive me and know you're included as well:

| | | |
|---|---|---|
| Biscuit | Lady | Frisky |
| Rascal | Silver | Sam |
| Rufus | Sambo | |

# *Some Final Musings...*

Live each day to the fullest—fill it with generous sprinkles of love, laughter, kindness, humility, and joy. Every day is a precious gift from God.

Take good care of yourself—eat healthily, get proper physical exercise, meditate and pray, and pamper yourself occasionally—you deserve it!

Celebrate the special person you are. Whatever your chronological age, enjoy life to the fullest instead of wasting time wishing you were twenty years younger or twenty years older. Each age brings its own challenges, adventures, and triumphs—don't miss out on any of them! And remember—in our hearts, we are all the same age.

Always listen to that small voice within you. Always go with your intuition—your "gut feeling." It is your heart speaking to you through your Higher Power and you *must* listen to it—it will not lead you astray.

Don't take life so seriously! Live outside the box. Take some risks. Get your hands a little dirty every now and then. Take the road less traveled once in a while and enjoy the scenery. Laugh a lot. Love a lot. Cry when you need to. Feel all your feelings all the time and enjoy life in living color every day.

Eliminate the words "always," "never," and "should" from your vocabulary. Nothing in this life is ever completely black or completely white—there are just many shades of gray. And stop telling yourself you "should" be doing something. Do those things that bring you joy and contentment and say "no" to all the rest.

Above all, remember that life isn't about comparisons. Don't compare yourself to anyone else—ever! You are a unique person, made up of many parts—some of them wonderful and some of them flawed. Work on your flaws but don't ever forget to celebrate the special person you are. You are good enough just the way you are right now. You are a work in progress so give yourself permission to enjoy every single minute of this exciting journey you're on.

# *To My Readers...*

Thank you for reading my little book and for letting me share so many of my thoughts and feelings with you. I hope it has enlightened you and that in some small way it has given you the inner strength and courage you need to start living your life to the fullest, beginning today!

For me, writing this book has been a labor of love and a wonderful experience. It has been both cathartic and freeing—cathartic because it has allowed me put so many of my thoughts and feelings down on paper, and freeing because I have had the courage to share much of my life with you, and that will allow me to move ahead to the next phase—whatever that may be!

I wish each of you Godspeed as you continue on the journey that is your life.

# Bibliography

The books listed in this section are the ones that are mentioned in my book.

[See also: "Suggested Readings," which provides a more comprehensive list of books, arranged by category.]

Beattie, Melody. *Codependent No More—How to Stop Controlling Others and Start Caring for Yourself.* San Francisco: Harper & Row, 1987.

—. *Beyond Codependency—and getting better all the time.* San Francisco: Harper & Row, 1989.

Cameron, Julia. *The Artist's Way—A Spiritual Path to Higher Creativity.* New York: Jeremy P. Tarcher/Putnam, 2002.

Cloud, Henry, Ph.D., and John Townsend, Ph.D. *Boundaries—When to say YES—When to Say NO—To Take Control of Your Life.* Grand Rapids: Zondervan, 1992.

Frankl, Viktor E. *Man's Search for Meaning* (Revised and Updated). New York: Washington Square Press, 1984.

Koch, Ruth N., and Kenneth C. Haugk. *Speaking the Truth in Love—How to Be an Assertive Christian.* St. Louis: Stephen Ministries, 1992.

Kübler-Ross, Elisabeth, M.D. *On Death and Dying—What the dying have to teach doctors, nurses, clergy, and their own family.* New York: Simon & Schuster, 1997.

Kushner, Harold. *When All You've Ever Wanted Isn't Enough—The Search for a Life That Matters.* New York: Simon & Schuster, 1986.

McGovern, George. *Terry.* New York: Penguin Group, 1996.

Morgenstern, Julie. *Organizing from the Inside Out—The Foolproof System for Organizing Your Home, Your Office, and Your Life.* New York: Henry Holt and Co., 1998.

Paulus, Trina. *hope for the flowers*. New York: Paulist Press, 1972.

Powell, John, S.J. *Why Am I Afraid to Tell You Who I Am?—Insights into Personal Growth*. Allen, TX: Thomas More, 1969.

Schultz, Charles. *Me, Stressed Out?* San Francisco: CollinsPublishers, 1996.

*Webster's II New College Dictionary*. Boston: Houghton Mifflin Co., 1995.

# Suggested Readings

✦

## (by category)

[In addition to the books listed in the Bibliography, the books listed below have helped me at various times over the years. This is by no means a comprehensive list (that simply isn't possible!), but I am personally familiar with all these books and I can recommend them without reservation. For more books in all these categories, please check with your local Library or bookstore.]

## Addictions

Fairburn, Christopher G., Dr. *Overcoming Binge Eating*. New York: The Guilford Press, 1995.

Kreisman, Jerold J., and Hal Straus. *I Hate You—don't leave me—Understanding the Borderline Personality*. New York: Avon Books, 1989.

Roth, Geneen. *When Food Is Love—Exploring the Relationship between Eating and Intimacy*. New York: Penguin Group, 1991.

Sheppard, Kay. *Food Addiction—The Body Knows*. Deerfield Beach, FL: Health Communications, Inc., 1993.

## Codependency

Alberti, Robert, and Michael Emmons. *Your Perfect Right—A Guide To Assertive Living* (Seventh Edition). San Luis Obispo, CA: Impact Publishers, 1995.

Beattie, Melody. *Playing It by Heart—Taking Care of Yourself No Matter What*. Center City, MN: Hazelden, 1999.

Bower, Sharon Anthony, and Gordon H. Bower. *Asserting Yourself—A Practical Guide for Positive Change.* Reading, MA: Perseus Books, 1991.

Hemfelt, Robert, Dr., Dr. Franklin Minirth, and Dr. Paul Meier. *Love Is a Choice—The Ground-breaking Book on Recovery for Codependent Relationships.* Nashville: Thomas Nelson Publishers, 1989.

Miller, J. Keith. *Compelled to Control—Recovering Intimacy in Broken Relationships.* Deerfield Beach, FL: Health Communications, Inc., 1992.

## Depression

Bloomfield, Harold H., M.D., and Peter McWilliams. *How to Heal Depression.* Los Angeles: Prelude Press, 1994.

Papolos, Demitri, M.D., and Janice Papolos. *Overcoming Depression—The Definitive Resource for Patients and Families Who Live with Depression and Manic-Depression.* New York: Harper Perennial, 1997.

## Fear

Jampolsky, Gerald G., M.D. *Love Is Letting Go of Fear.* Berkeley: Celestial Arts, 1979.

Jeffers, Susan, Ph.D. *Feel the Fear and Do It Anyway—Dynamic techniques for turning fear, indecision, and anger into power, action, and love.* New York: Fawcett Columbine, 1987.

Quigly, Sarah (with Marilyn Shroyer, Ph.D.). *Facing Fear, Finding Courage—Your Path To Peace of Mind.* Berkeley: Conari Press, 1996.

## Grief/Death and Dying

Beattie, Melody. *The Lessons of Love—Rediscovering Our Passion for Life When It All Seems Too Hard To Take.* San Francisco: Harper Collins, 1994.

Bockelman, Wilfred. *Finding the Right Words—Offering Care & Comfort When You Don't Know What to Say.* Minneapolis: Augsburg, 1990.

Callanan, Maggie, and Patricia Kelley. *Final Gifts—Understanding the Special Awareness, Needs, and Communications of the Dying.* New York: Bantam Books, 1997.

DelBene, Ron (with Mary and Herb Montgomery). *A Time to Mourn—Recovering from the Death of a Loved One.* Nashville: The Upper Room, 1998.

James, John W., and Russell Friedman. *The Grief Recovery Handbook—The Action Program for Moving Beyond Death, Divorce, and Other Losses.* New York: Harper Collins, 1998.

Lambin, Helen R. *From Grief to Grace—Images for Overcoming Sadness and Loss.* Chicago: ACTA Publications, 1997.

Lewis, C. S. *A Grief Observed.* New York: Bantam Books, 1961.

Linn, Erin. *I Know Just How You Feel...avoiding the cliches of grief.* Incline Village, NV: The Publisher's Mark, 1986.

Maxwell, Katie. *Bedside Manners—A Practical Guide To Visiting the Ill.* Grand Rapids: Baker Book House Co., 1990.

Miller, James E. *Winter Grief, Summer Grace—Returning to Life After a Loved One Dies.* Minneapolis: Augsburg, 1995.

Moore, James W. *When Grief Breaks Your Heart.* Nashville: Abingdon Press, 1995.

Sittser, Gerald L. *A Grace Disguised—How the Soul Grows Through Loss.* Grand Rapids: Zondervan Publishing House, 1995.

Smith, Harold Ivan. *A Decembered Grief—Living with Loss While Others Are Celebrating.* Kansas City: Beacon Hill Press, 1999.

Tatelbaum, Judy. *The Courage to Grieve—Creative Living, Recovery, & Growth Through Grief.* New York: Harper & Row, 1980.

Van Praagh, James. *Healing Grief—Reclaiming Life After Any Loss*. New York: Penguin Group, 2000.

Westberg, Granger E. *Good Grief.* Minneapolis: Fortress Press, 1997.


## Humor

Cousins, Norman. *Anatomy of an Illness—as Perceived by the Patient*. New York: Bantam Books, 1979.

Klein, Allen. *The Healing Power of Humor—Techniques for Getting through Loss, Setbacks, Upsets, Disappointments, Difficulties, Trials, Tribulations, and All That Not-So-Funny Stuff.* New York: Jeremy P. Tarcher/Putnam, 1989.


## Meditation Books

Anon. *A New Day—365 Meditations for Personal and Spiritual Growth*. Toronto: Bantam Books, 1989.

Beattie, Melody. *The Language of Letting Go—Daily Meditations for Codependents*. New York: Harper Collins, 1990.

—. *More Language of Letting Go*. Center City, MN: Hazelden, 2000.

Lerner, Rockelle. *Affirmations for the Inner Child*. Deerfield Beach, FL: Health Communications, Inc., 1990.

Powell, John, S.J. *Through Seasons of the Heart*. Allen, TX: Thomas More, 1987.

Ryan, M. J. *Attitudes of Gratitude—How to Give and Receive Joy Every Day of Your Life*. Berkeley: Conari Press, 1999.

Schaef, Anne Wilson. *Meditations for People Who Worry*. New York: Ballantine Publishing Group, 1996.

Voigt, Anna. *Simple Meditations—for everyday relaxation and rejuvenation*. New York: Barnes & Noble Books, 2001.

## Recovery

Bradshaw, John. *Homecoming—Reclaiming and Championing Your Inner Child.* New York: Bantam Books, 1990.

—. *Creating Love—The Next Great Stage of Growth.* New York: Bantam Books, 1992.

Fiore, Neil, Ph.D. *Overcoming Procrastination—Practice the Now Habit and Guilt-Free Play.* New York: MJF Books, 1989.

Hay, Louise L. *You Can Heal Your Life.* Carson, CA: Hay House, Inc., 1987.

John-Roger, and Peter McWilliams. *You Can't Afford the Luxury of a Negative Thought—A Book for People with Any Life-Threatening Illness—Including Life.* Los Angeles: Prelude Press, Inc., 1988.

Kabat-Zinn, Jon, Ph.D. *Full Catastrophe Living—Using the Wisdom of Your Body and Mind to Face Stress, Pain, and Illness.* New York: Delta Publishing, 1990.

Smedes, Lewis B. *Shame and Grace—Healing the Shame We Don't Deserve.* San Francisco: Zondervan Publishing House, 1993.

Twerski, Abraham J., M.D. *Waking Up Just in Time—A therapist shows how to use the Twelve Steps approach to life's ups and downs.* New York: St. Martin's Griffin, 1990.

Weedn, Flavia, and Lisa Weedn. *To Take Away the Hurt—Insights to Healing.* San Rafael, CA: Cedco Publishing Co., 1999.

Whitfield, Charles L., M.D. *Healing the Child Within—Discovery and Recovery for Adult Children of Dysfunctional Families.* Deerfield Beach, FL: Health Communications, Inc., 1987.

## Self-Improvement

Freeman, Arthur, Dr., and Rose DeWolf. *Woulda, Coulda, Shoulda—Overcoming Regrets, Mistakes, and Missed Opportunities.* New York: Harper Collins, 1989.

—. *The 10 Dumbest Mistakes Smart People Make and How to Avoid Them—Simple and Sure Techniques for Gaining Greater Control of Your Life*. New York: Harper Collins, 1992.

McMahon, Susanna, Ph.D. *The Portable Therapist—Wise and Inspiring Answers to the Questions People in Therapy Ask Most...*New York: Dell Trade Paperback, 1992.

Powell, John, S.J., and Loretta Brady, M.S.W. *Will The Real Me Please Stand Up?—25 Guidelines for Good Communication*. Allen, TX: Thomas More, 1985.

Salzberg, Sharon. *LovingKindness—The Revolutionary Art of Happiness*. Boston: Shambhala, 1997.

Sullivan, James E. *The Good Listener*. Notre Dame, IN: Ave Maria Press, 2000.

Thurman, Chris, Dr. *The Lies We Believe—The #1 Cause of Our Unhappiness*. Nashville: Thomas Nelson Publishers, 1989.

Spirituality

Albom, Mitch. *tuesdays with Morrie—an old man, a young man, and life's greatest lesson*. New York: Doubleday, 1997.

Fann, Joey. *The Way Back to Mayberry—Lessons from a Simpler Time*. Nashville: Broadman & Holman Publishers, 2001.

Halberstam, Yitta, and Judith Leventhal. *Small Miracles—Extraordinary Coincidences from Everyday Life*. Holbrook, MA: Adams Media Corp., 1997.

Heatherly, Joyce Landorf. *Balcony People*. Austin, TX: Balcony Publishing, 1984.

Kushner, Harold S. *When Bad Things Happen To Good People*. New York: Avon Books, 1981.

—. *How Good Do We Have to Be?* Boston: Little, Brown and Co., 1996.

Mother Teresa. *No Greater Love*. Novato, CA: New World Library, 1997.

Peck, M. Scott, M.D. *The Road Less Traveled—A New Psychology of Love, Traditional Values and Spiritual Growth.* New York: Simon & Schuster, 1978.

—. *Further Along The Road Less Traveled—The Unending Journey Toward Spiritual Growth—The Edited Lectures.* New York: Simon & Schuster, 1993.

—. *The Road Less Traveled & Beyond—Spiritual Growth in an Age of Anxiety.* New York: Simon & Schuster, 1997.

Youngs, Bettie B., Ph.D. *a String of Pearls—Inspirational stories celebrating the resiliency of the human spirit.* Holbrook, MA: Adams Media Corp., 2000.

## Women's Issues

Baer, Jean. *How To Be an Assertive (not Aggressive) Woman—In Life, In Love, and On the Job—The Classic Guide to Becoming a Self-assured Person.* New York: Penguin Group, 1976.

Covington, Stephanie S., Ph.D. *A Woman's Way through the Twelve Steps.* Center City, MN: Hazelden, 1994.

Lerner, Harriet, Ph.D. *The Dance of Anger—A Woman's Guide To Changing the Patterns of Intimate Relationships.* New York: Harper & Row Publishers, 1985.

—. *The Dance of Intimacy—A Woman's Guide To Courageous Acts of Change in Key Relationships.* New York: Harper & Row Publishers, 1989.

—. *The Dance of Deception—A Guide to Authenticity and Truth-Telling in Women's Relationships.* New York: Quill, 1993.

LeSound, Sandra Simpson. *The Not-So-Compulsive Woman—20 Recovery Principles to Pull You Out of the Pit.* Tarrytown, NY: Chosen Books, 1992.

Reilly, Patricia Lynn. *Imagine a Woman in Love with Herself—Embracing Your Wisdom and Wholeness.* Berkeley: Conari Press, 1999.

Williamson, Marianne. *A Woman's Worth.* New York: Ballantine Books, 1993.

Miscellaneous

Canfield, Jack, and Mark Victor Hansen. *The Aladdin Factor*. New York: Berkley Books, 1995.

Carlson, Richard, Ph.D. *Don't sweat the small stuff...and it's all small stuff—Simple Ways to Keep the Little Things from Taking Over Your Life*. New York: Hyperion, 1997.

*Emanuel's Book—A manual for living comfortably in the cosmos*. Compiled by Pat Rodegast and Judith Stanton. New York: Bantam Books, 1987.

0-595-27402-1